The
POWER
of little words

Some Ideas
to Improve Your Writing

by John L. Beckley

Illustrated by Jean Crane

Published by The Economics Press, Inc.
12 Daniel Road, Fairfield, N.J. 07006

Additional copies are available at $14.95 each (plus postage)
from The Economics Press, 12 Daniel Rd., Fairfield, N.J. 07006.
Or call toll free: 1-800-526-2554 (in N.J., 1-800-526-1128).

ISBN 0-910187-02-9
Printed in the United States of America

Table of Contents

Hello!

This is not a book for scholars. Scholars live way out in the wild blue yonder of the mind, an area mostly out of touch with reality.

Neither is it a book for would-be dramatists, novelists, or poets. Some of the ideas it contains might be useful to such people, but it is certainly not being written with them in mind.

My idea is simply to compile a practical book for anyone who wishes to learn how to express his or her ideas more clearly, and with greater interest to the reader. There is nothing artistic or literary about it—unless you happen to believe, as I do, that the lucid and compelling expression of ideas is an art in itself.

Writing and editing have been my life. One of my more egocentric pleasures is to pick up a piece of writing I did some years ago and discover that I would say it exactly the same way today. Quite honestly, that rarely happens. The ability to express oneself, like any other talent, improves with time and practice.

Over years of writing—and reading other writers—I have noticed that professional writers observe and practice many principles that less experienced writers seem totally unaware of. That's what this book is about. If you are interested in improving your writing, you may find some of them quite helpful.

Conversational English
vs.
Written English

English is not just one language; it's two languages.

One is spoken English—the plain, ordinary words and simple sentence structures we use in talking with friends and acquaintances. The other language is written English, the more complicated words and sentences most people use when they try to put something in writing.

Conversational English is informal. There's nothing pretentious about it whatsoever. The sole purpose is to convey information, to make the speaker's facts and feelings as easy as possible to understand. Usually, the speaker is totally relaxed and is not trying to impress anyone in the process.

Written English, unfortunately, often has other purposes. The most common one is to impress the reader with the brains, culture, and abilities of the writer. The pure, clean purpose of giving the reader accurate information in a form he can most easily handle is obscured. Written English has a strong tendency to serve the ego of the writer rather than the interests of the reader.

People loosen up when they talk to a close personal friend. They express ideas in a much more relaxed, interesting manner than when they try to write something down. The minute a great many people have to put something in writing they begin to worry about being "on the record" and what others may think of them. It makes their language tense, formal, and stuffy.

Most of us have learned from experience that we have to talk simply and directly to our friends in order to be understood. If we don't talk simply, nobody bothers to listen—they can't follow what we're saying. That's why we automatically turn to shorter sentences, simpler construction, and shorter, more familiar words.

Simplicity in conversation is such an automatic requirement we take it for granted. If we're talking to someone and express an idea in complicated form, the listener's face goes blank. We can see that he isn't following us. So we stop, even in mid-sentence, and try a new tack. We don't worry about complete sentences the way we do when we write. We interject explanatory remarks right in the middle of a sentence. When we find ourselves using a complicated word, we repeat the same idea using a simpler word.

We all talk this way with our friends, but very few of us write this way. Why not? Because most of us have been taught not to from our very earliest English class right on through college. The emphasis in education is rarely placed on communicating ideas simply and clearly. Instead we're encouraged to use more complicated words and sentence structures to show off our learning and literacy. As far as the needs of the average person are concerned, the kind of writing instruction most of us have gotten in school is exactly the reverse of what we need. Instead of teaching us how to communicate as clearly as possible, our schooling in English teaches us how to fog things up. It even implants a fear that if we don't make our writing complicated enough, we'll be considered uneducated.

Strangely enough, this is especially true among candidates for graduate degrees. Advanced students are often warned that, if they want to make the grade, they'll have to learn to express their ideas in more complicated, professional language. Stuffy, impressive sounding wordage has become a benchmark of scholarship. Who cares if you could say the same thing more simply and clearly and more people would understand it? Go peddle your papers!

The people who are most aware of the drawbacks of stuffy, schoolbook, scholarly English are the professional writers. The professionals are well aware that a conversational, easy-to-read, interesting style will bring them more readers, wider circulation, and more money. Every important, popular magazine or newspaper in America features conversational, easy-to-read articles. None of them use scholarly, schoolbook English.

What many language teachers have never stopped to appreciate is that famous writers of the past used a conversational style too—reasonably short sentences and mostly familiar words. This includes John Bunyan, Samuel Pepys, Daniel Defoe, and Jonathan Swift. Also American writers like Franklin, Emerson, Thoreau, and Mark Twain. What distinguishes great writers is not their vocabulary or scholarly phraseology. What marks them as outstanding is what they have to say and the clarity and interest with which they say it.

The best, clearest writing is not impersonal. It always sounds like someone talking. Do the sentences you have written sound like you? If not, put them aside and start over. As Rudolph Flesch said in *The Art of Readable Writing:* "We write stilted English because we unconsciously assume that this is what is expected of us in the

9

position we happen to fill or the organization we belong to." In other words, because we are pretending to be something we are not.

You will do your best writing when you are trying to sound exactly like you, not like someone else. When you're copying others, saying things and expressing ideas in language that isn't really yours, the fakery is obvious. On the other hand, if you are trying to be yourself, and your head works a little differently and more interestingly than other people's heads, you may be sensational.

One of the things that will help make your writing sound like conversation is to use contractions just like you do when you are talking: "He won't" "She isn't". Keep your sentences short. Express a piece of an idea at a time—don't try to jam the whole thing into one complex sentence. Use shorter, common words, eliminate longer, uncommon ones. When you use a more difficult word, use other, familiar expressions with it—or explain it—so people can easily grasp its meaning. For example: "She was very perspicacious—nobody could fool her." "It happened simultaneously—at the same instant." Use short comments and insert partial sentences when they will help make the meaning clear.

Say things before you write them. Do they sound natural and relaxed, the way you would tell them to an old friend? After you've finished writing, read the result aloud. Does it sound smooth and flow easily as you read it? Does it really sound like you talking? If it does, fine—let it stand. Don't worry for a minute about what anyone is going to think of you. Write to express, not to impress. Bowl people over with the clarity of your thought and imagery, not the stuffiness of your manner.

People are often amused if they walk into my office when I'm tackling a tough piece of writing. There I am, sitting at the typewriter talking and gesturing to no one in particular. What they don't realize is that I'm talking to Joe, an invisible friend who sits directly in front of me, across the typewriter. Everything I write, I try out on Joe first. I have to explain things carefully and be sure he understands. I don't dare use unnecessarily complicated terms or he'll think I'm getting stuck up and trying to show off. Joe keeps me human and down to earth. I can tell, by listening carefully as I talk to him and imagining his reaction, whether or not I'm on target.

It's not easy to learn to write simply and unpretentiously. As you get the hang of it though, you'll find the quality of your writing will improve noticeably. Good writers seem to get better and better; they mature with experience. The uncertainty is gone. They are completely confident, sitting and talking with the reader just as they have done so successfully many times before. Their writing, as a result, becomes more and more a pleasure to read.

Why Write So Simply?

Well, there you have it—the most important single idea in this book. Write simply and conversationally. Use the same language you would use in talking to a close friend.

But why write so simply? Isn't it a bit childish? Isn't a large vocabulary of any use whatsoever?

Yes, it is. But primarily to help you read and understand others, especially those who aren't skillful enough to present their ideas more simply. When you use shorter, more common words, and shorter sentences, it doesn't mean you're writing baby talk. What it means is that you're making it easier for a lot more people to understand what you're driving at. More people will try to read what you have written instead of throwing it in the wastebasket.

Writing so you can be easily understood is more of a problem these days than most people realize. The reading ability of the American public has dropped so sharply in the last 50 years it's almost unbelievable. If you are a good reader—and especially if you learned to read a good many years ago—you may have little idea what poor readers most people are today. We seldom hear other people read aloud. Mostly they read quietly and in private. If you could hear them read aloud, you might be just as shocked as one of my associates recently was.

My friend, Jean, is a professional writer and has been for years. She enjoys having lunch occasionally with her niece, an intelligent, interesting, college graduate who is now in her mid-thirties. The other day the niece pulled out a clipping she wanted to read to Jean. She proceeded to do so, haltingly, one word at a time, with obvious difficulty. Jean was shocked. She couldn't believe it.

If you could hear some of the people you know read aloud, you wouldn't believe it either.

The number of Americans who can't read has become a national disgrace—something the Russians and other critics make great fun of. The U.S. Office of Education reports that more than 23,000,000 Americans (one out of ten) can't read the simplest sort of things, like safety signs, want ads, and labels on boxes and bottles. And it isn't because they didn't go to school—five out of six of the people who can't read have had more than three years of schooling. Our efforts to teach them to read have been a total failure.

In the last 20 years the reading scores of people seeking entrance to college have dropped 10 percent. Millions of children now enter high school with what used to be fifth grade reading ability. Reading ability has declined so much we've had to simplify high school and college textbooks. Otherwise students couldn't read well enough to understand them. Newspapers and magazines also have to be written more simply than they used to be or people won't read them.

Why do I mention the reading crisis in a book on writing? Because every time I talk about the importance of keeping things simple, I can see the intellectuals who like to use more complicated language stiffening in their chairs with disapproval. Personally, I prefer to keep things simple anyway. These days, however, it happens to be a necessity. The American people are having a terrific communications problem. Most of the people we write for can't read well; some of them can barely read at all.

You might like to reach these people, whether they read your books, magazines, advertisements, or the memoranda you post on the bulletin board. It will help you do so if you understand a little more about their problems.

Why should elementary school students in European countries be able to read two or three times as many words as our children? Most people tend to blame television. But television is a Johnny-come-lately. The reading ability of our school children started sagging long before there was a television set in every living room. The reason for our troubles, many critics believe, is that the schools changed their method of teaching children how to read. That happened back in the 1930's and 1940's.

Until 1930 the traditional method of teaching reading was to teach phonics first, the sounds represented by various letters and letter combinations. People were always drilled in phonics first when they learned to read. This was true, not only in the United States, but in every country that used an alphabet to reproduce its language in written form.

In the late 1920's, however, America's reading experts— the college professors who wrote the reading texts and instructed teachers how to teach reading—became dissatisfied with the "phonics first" method. They said it was too dull. Why introduce children to such an exciting, important subject as reading by forcing them to spend months memorizing the sounds of so many letters and letter combinations? Why not start them immediately on stories containing a few simple words they could learn to recognize on sight without worrying about the sounds of letters and syllables?

Another thing they objected to was sounding out words in order to recognize them. Experienced readers, especially speed readers, don't sound out syllables when they read. They don't pronounce the words, even mentally. They recognize the meaning of words and groups of words on sight. If that is the ultimate goal—to sense the meaning of written words on sight—why not teach reading that way from the very beginning? Don't bother with sounds and syllables; teach children to recognize words on sight.

They called the new method "look-say". It was strictly theoretical, still not tested enough to be sure how it would work. Nevertheless, the ideas were so appealing to leading intellectuals in the reading business that the idea swept the country.

Almost immediately, severe reading problems began to appear and multiply. So did problems with spelling. Strangely enough, nobody of any professional consequence attributed these problems to the new teaching method. Educators thought they must be due to nervous and physical problems inherent in the children. Complex studies were made to try to discover what these ailments were and how to treat them.

Eventually, in 1955, a bomb exploded. An outsider to the reading profession, Dr. Rudolph Flesch, brought out a book entitled *WHY JOHNNY CAN'T READ*. "The teaching of reading," said Flesch, "all over the United States, in all the schools, and in all the textbooks is totally wrong and flies in the face of all logic and common sense." He urged a return to phonics first.

Flesch was not a specialist in teaching reading. If he had

been, he might have been afraid to criticize the hierarchy of his profession so brazenly. Flesch had, however, written a number of important, highly respected books about how to write. He was also a prominent consultant to newspapers, magazines, and press associations on how to improve the readability of their publications.

The reading and educational authorities, however, didn't give an inch. Flesch's book had little effect in the nation's schoolrooms. A few courageous school districts went back to teaching phonics first and a few reading specialists eventually came out and publicly agreed with Flesch. But most school districts simply kept on doing what they had been doing—teaching look-say. Remedial problems kept increasing and the nation's reading ability kept sliding.

More than 25 years later, in 1981, Flesch fired another cannonball, this one called *Why Johnny Still Can't Read*. In this book he took apart, piece by piece, the arguments his opposition had used. Every valid, impartial test, Flesch claimed, showed that phonics first was a more effective way to teach reading than look-say. Phonics first gave the child a tool he could use and trust to recognize new words and recall old ones. Look-say, on the other hand, was a guessing game. It destroyed children's confidence in themselves and their ability to learn. There was no sense to it, just sheer memory. Too many words—without the sounds to guide one—looked just like other words. Sight recognition of words and phrases should come later, after a student had read them thousands of times, not when he was just learning to read.

It's hard to believe that a controversy over the methods of teaching reading—the most vital subject in our educational system—could rage for more than 50 years. Yet it has, and it still isn't settled. Why not? Why can't impartial scientists (not reading professors) make some indisputable, fact-finding tests that will end the bickering? Even though victims who can't read are piled up all around us, we still can't agree how it happened and why it keeps on happening.

To you, as a writer, this situation has a very clear message. If you want to reach many readers, don't get flowery or complex. Keep it simple. Even if we corrected the situation immediately—and there is no sign that we will—the damage has already been done. Millions and millions of people who can't read very well will be with us for the next 10 to 60 years. Give a thought to them every time you sit down to write.

What Makes Writing Readable?

People who have studied the readability of various pieces of writing agree that two things are vital. One is the length of the sentences. The other is the length and familiarity of the words. Short sentences and short, familiar words are much easier to read than longer, more complex ones.

In trying to create an index by which one can measure readability, these two factors are often combined into one by counting the number of syllables per sentence. The more words, and the more complex the words, the more syllables there will be in the average sentence.

If you'd like to measure the readability of your writing, you can dig out one of the books by Gunning or Flesch and figure out your rating. What's more important, however, is to be conscious of what will make your writing more readable and start doing it. Stick to simpler words. Eliminate complicated ways of saying things that require more words. Don't try to shove too many ideas into a single sentence. Establish the basic idea in one sentence, then add to and elaborate on it in the next sentence.

Does simple sentence structure mean your writing is juvenile? No, it certainly doesn't. Anything but. Look, for example, at the following quote from an editorial that appeared in a business magazine. It's on a very complicated subject, economics, written for a well-informed audience of business executives. To reach the average audience, the words would have to be simpler. But look at the sentences. The amazing thing about this editorial is the simplicity and directness of its sentence structure. No complex sentences. And in every compound sentence the second thought follows easily after the first in natural, logical sequence.

> *"This has been a time of grand visions for the economy— some optimistic, some pessimistic. We have heard proposals for 'reindustrialization.' We have been told about structural shifts that are carrying us along to a service economy. We have heard of the death of basic industries—and of their renaissance.*
>
> *"Whatever school of thought we embrace, we can be misled about the essential truth of what is going on. Sweeping visions of what is happening tend to make us think that mystical laws of economics will shape the days ahead— that we should wait to see what is in store for us.*
>
> *"This has also been a time of criticism of American management, with much of the criticism coming from within its own ranks. Healthy self-analysis can be constructive. But, if we wallow in self-blame, the effort can be destructive to individual companies and to the nation."*

Perhaps I shouldn't have used an example that contains such difficult concepts. What I was trying to demonstrate is that direct, uncomplicated sentence structure is used by good writers at every level. There's nothing amateurish or unsophisticated about it.

In reproducing the above message, however, I began to wonder how it would sound if the writer had used simpler words. Please note that I am concerned with how it would *sound*, not with how it would *read*. If something *sounds* well, it will automatically *read* well.

Here it is, using somewhat simpler wordage:

"*This has been a time of grand predictions for business—some good, some bad. Some people propose rebuilding our basic industries. Others forecast a shift in emphasis from manufacturing products to delivering services—computer and communications services for example. We hear that basic industries are dying—then others report they're reviving.*

"*Whatever school of thought we embrace, we can easily be misled. Sweeping predictions of what will happen tend to make us think that mystical laws of economics are shaping the days ahead. All we need do is wait and watch it take place.*

"*American management has been criticized, with much of the criticism coming from its own ranks. That's not bad—it's good. But enough is enough. If we wallow in self-criticism, it can be bad for individual companies and the country as well.*"

Did you notice any difference in readability? I think it's at least a little easier to grasp.

Why do businesspeople turn their backs on the simple, direct way of writing things in favor of more pompous, stilted language? Probably to show each other how smart they are, and to sound like the thousands of businesspeople who did it before them.

The associates of Richard Morris, a nationally-known business writing consultant, once analyzed more than 3,000,000 business letters. "At least half of the business communications mailed daily are twice as long as they should be," they concluded. "Many are so full of technical and legal jargon, and so repetitious, that most people cannot understand them."

Have you ever received a letter, or seen a letter, from a person who is already so successful that he or she no longer bothers to try to impress anybody? We've seen a few such letters. Invariably they are relaxed, short, and simple— shockingly so when compared with the average letter.

Glenn Kerfoot, The Letter Doctor of Lexington, KY, described the wordiness disease in *Keep It Simple*, a little booklet he wrote some years ago. His analysis is so amusing I asked his permission to reproduce it here.

Marty Phillips, a manager in a large manufacturing firm, asked his secretary to distribute supplies of a new report form to each of his foremen.

The girl delivered part of the forms personally, telling each foreman she saw: "If you need more of these forms, call me." Then she prepared the rest of the forms for mail distribution. Laboriously, Marty composed a memo to send along with them. It read: "In the event that you are desirous of obtaining additional supplies of the enclosed form, kindly contact this office at your earliest convenience."

Marty handled this simple writing chore in a way that is common in business today. Instead of writing: "If you need more of these forms, call me," he buried a simple idea under pompous, elaborate language.

Unfortunately, many people in business think they have to write this way. New employees adopt the habits of the old-timers, and a vicious circle of poor communication results.

No one says that business writers should adopt the one-syllable vocabulary of the first-grade student. However, simple writing can have genuine strength and dignity, and still be understandable. The Lord's Prayer has endured for centuries, though it is written in language a child can understand.

Take a look at some of the great statements of history—phrases uttered in the heat of battle by men who wanted to communicate, not confuse. "Don't fire until you see the white of their eyes." . . . "Damn the torpedoes! Full speed ahead." . . . "These are the times that try men's souls." . . . and that World War II classic of conciseness, "Sighted sub. Sank same."

Clarity alone may not account for the enduring popularity of statements like "Don't give up the ship!" but it's doubtful that Lawrence's remark would be printed in every history book if he had said, "Please be advised to retain control of this vessel until further notice."

Business letters, memos, and reports contain far too much fancy, abstract language—too many big words—too many long, windy phrases. The people who write this way know what they're talking about—but they don't say it.

In business writing, things rarely get started anymore. Instead they are "activated", "instigated", "initiated", or "inaugurated". New policies are "implemented". Equipment is not used, but "utilized". A friendly call is a "visitation".

Managers don't think—they "philosophize". They don't try something; rather they "attempt" or "endeavor". They don't find out things—they "ascertain". Instead of helping someone, they "render assistance". They don't get things—they "secure" or "obtain" them. They see only the things that are "readily discernible".

Business-letter writers don't just know something; they are "cognizant of the fact that. . . ." Something that is proper is "appropriate", and facts must always be "pertinent".

A man is no longer paid for his work. Instead, he is "compensated", "remunerated", or "reimbursed". Things don't even end anymore—they are "terminated" or "finalized", they're "completed", or "concluded".

Henry Watson Fowler, the grand old man of English usage, once said, "Those who run to long words are mainly the unskillful and tasteless. They confuse pomposity with dignity, and bulk with force."

The fellow who thinks he needs big words to express a simple thought or idea is wasteful. He wastes his own time and the time of the people who must understand and use his communications. The habitual user of big words and fancy language, unfortunately, is more interested in impressing people than in expressing thoughts.

Short Words

Why do short words make for easier readability?

Because almost everyone recognizes them on sight. The meaning is perceived instantaneously. Also, perhaps because people use them constantly in conversation, they seem to have more force and meaning.

Technical reading experts may have more complicated reasons why shorter words can be understood more quickly. Whatever the reasons, it's an observable fact. Take a look, for example, at the following list of words. The more complicated word is on the left, the simpler one on the right. Even though you understand all the words, which most readers will, which one strikes you as conveying the meaning more clearly and forcefully?

abundance	plenty
above mentioned	this
acquire	get, gain
advantageous	helpful
advise	say, tell
anticipate	expect, look for
approximate	about
ascertain	find out
available	ready
assistance	help, aid
commence	begin, start
competent	able
comprised	made up of
concerning	about

conclusion	end
cursory	short
determine	find out
difficult	hard
efficacy	effectiveness
eliminate	wipe out, omit
endeavor	try
explicit	clear, plain
exceedingly	very
expedite	hasten
facilitate	make easy
furnish	give
henceforth	after this
forthwith	now, at once
inasmuch as	since
initial	first
institute	begin
interior	inside
maintenance	upkeep
necessitate	force
negligent	careless
participate	share in
peruse, perusal	study
possess	have
procure	get
preserve	keep
prominent	leading
provide	give
pursuant to	according to
remunerate	pay
relinquish	give up
render	give
restrict	limit
retain	keep

secure	get
solution	answer
sufficient	enough
terminate	end
ultimate	final
withhold	hold back

I'm not recommending that you abandon the words in the left-hand columns above and never use them. What I mean to point out is this: If you tend to use the words in the left-hand column more frequently than those in the right, your communications are losing force and clarity. Whenever you want something to be extremely clear, or a letter seems a little stuffy or wordy, take a look at the words you've used. Start replacing the longer, less common words with shorter, simpler expressions. Look for plain, ordinary, conversational words that give an immediate, sharp impression.

Some people may suspect that we're trying to impoverish the English language by cutting down the number of words in use. We're not interested in that at all—learn all the words you care to. But when you really want to be understood, say things simply! It's the most effective way to express yourself, regardless of whether your message is going to top management or to the mail clerk.

Don't bother to try to remember the words in the above listing. That's only the beginning. There are thousands of other words that can be replaced by simpler, more forceful ones. Just remember the principle and apply it. Whenever your copy doesn't roll easily, whenever it seems tedious or foggy, take a look at the words you've used. Try substituting shorter, stronger ones and see if it doesn't help.

Single words can often be substituted for lengthy expressions containing a number of words. They express the idea just as well, forcefully, and save effort for the reader. For example:

at a later date	later
in the amount of	for
after which time	then
first and foremost	first
in the event that	if
be good enough to	please
with special regard to	as to
on the grounds that	since, because
for the purpose of	for, to
in the neighborhood of	about

When management and labor lock horns in a battle of public statements, management almost invariably comes off second best. Why? One obvious reason is that the labor leaders talk everybody's English. They know the people they want to reach and they talk the language those people think with. Company statements are written in executive-level, business English, mushy with unnecessary verbiage.

There is no reason to use more complex words, instead of simple ones, unless your goal is to impress people with how learned you are. Complex language will lose some readers completely, make it harder for others. It doesn't communicate ideas nearly as well. All it does is sound pretentious.

Simple language will *not* make anyone think you are writing down to them unless you actually are. Simple language gives the impression of great ease and clarity in your thought. Difficult concepts, particularly, benefit from simple language. The ability to express them simply is a sign of brilliance.

Short words are the quickest, most direct road to people's minds. Take advantage of them.

Periods Are Beautiful

Whenever I turn the page in a serious book (books of fiction don't count), I'm always relieved if the next one is broken into a number of paragraphs. Generally, the more paragraphs the better, although some promotional letter writers have carried this idea to a silly extreme. Virtually every sentence in their letter asking for money to defeat Senator Zilch is a separate paragraph.

But it must work. Somebody must have tested it and compared the results with an ordinary looking letter with normal sized paragraphs. How long it will continue to work is another question. I suspect it's a fad that will lose its effectiveness just as soon as readers get tired of it.

Nevertheless, the idea is based on a very sound principle: A great many readers dread a solid page of type. It's always wise, therefore, if you're concerned about keeping your audience with you, to sprinkle in three or four paragraphs per page, sometimes more. It breaks up the page of type. It indicates to the reader that there will be at least three or four places where he can relax, take a breath, and think things over.

The same thing is true of periods. As a reader starts a paragraph it's always encouraging to see a few periods ahead. That's where he knows he can stop and pull his thoughts together without losing anything in the process. I've noticed, in typing this section, that typists leave more space at the end of each sentence than typesetters do. After a period, a typist hits the space bar twice. Typesetters, unfortunately, run their sentences much closer together.

What they ought to do, after especially long sentences, is to print a symbol for a steaming cup of coffee. That would indicate to the reader that he could relax, have a sip of coffee, and go back and see if he could figure out what that last sentence was all about.

Most long sentences are not totally bewildering. Usually you can get some sense out of them. But they do make the meaning foggier and reading less enjoyable. Consider, for example, the following sentences from a book about how to teach reading.

> *"This particular concern for the quality of the reading program in our schools has, of course, always been with us even when there was every reason to believe that it was a good program, for there is nothing new about the fact that the ability to read well is the first requisite to obtaining a good education. But the reading program in our elementary schools now has a special significance that it never had before, not only because there is every reason to believe that it is an extremely poor program, as this book intends abundantly to demonstrate, but also because the national interest, including the national economy, is now more closely tied to our educational system than it has ever been before in this country's history."*

The sentences are so complex I'm not sure I get everything he is driving at. Everything I do understand, however could be presented more simply as follows:

> *"We have always been concerned about the quality of the reading program in our schools even when we were pretty sure it was a good one. The ability to read well is the first*

requirement for obtaining a good education.

Today people are more concerned than ever. Today's reading program is not teaching children to read as well as we used to read. As reading ability slips, the quality of our educational system is slipping with it. That is damaging to our national economy and other national interests."

With two paragraphs and six periods, I hope I have made it a little easier to read and understand than the writer did with one paragraph and two periods.

A sentence is a complete thought. That means it must contain at least two words, a subject which acts, or is acted upon, and a verb which expresses the action. There are one word sentences like "Go!" or "Stop!" but in those cases the subject *you* is understood. There can also be one word exclamations or comments like "Certainly." or "Tomorrow for sure." But those are not really sentences. A sentence has a subject and a verb. Unfortunately, it may also have independent clauses, subordinate clauses and phrases that run to hundreds of words. There's no law to stop the verbiage. As a writer you have a right to use as much as you want. But if you are the least bit interested in getting your meaning across to readers, short sentences are better than long ones.

How much can one sentence carry? It's a good idea not to put more in any one sentence than it can *easily* carry. If there is any doubt, break the thoughts into separate pieces and organize them as independent sentences in the most logical, easy to grasp order.

The period is the most valuable and neglected punctuation mark in the English language. Almost everyone could make his writing more clear, interesting, and readable by using more periods. Simple? Yes, but do it! It's one of the most vital suggestions we know for improving letters, reports, releases, and articles.

One of the most abused punctuation marks is the semicolon. Most people use it to separate independent clauses that are internally punctuated. Technically, they're absolutely right. As a practical matter, they're dead wrong. Most of the sentences in which they use semicolons are longish affairs that ought to be rewritten as two or more independent sentences. They ought to be separated by periods, not semicolons—it's easier on the reader.

The right use for a semicolon is to separate *short* independent clauses. A semicolon separates the two thoughts yet indicates that there is some relationship between the two. It is also less bumpy and staccato than a period. For example:

> John drinks milk; Mary likes coffee.
>
> Milk is plentiful; it's inexpensive too.

There may be times when you want the abrupt, staccato effect a period gives. If so, use it. Otherwise, a semicolon is smoother. The semicolon indicates some relationship between the two ideas.

Clarity, Clarity, Clarity

If any man wish to write in a clear style, let him be first clear in his thoughts.

Goethe

It isn't hard to write something which, if a person takes the time to study it, is absolutely clear. But writing that has to be studied is not a good communication. The meaning of good writing is so immediately clear and obvious it doesn't have to be studied.

Someone once wrote to a government bureau asking whether hydrochloric acid could be used to clean the tubes in his steam boiler. He received this reply.

Uncertainties of reactive processes make the use of hydrochloric acid undesirable where alkalinity is involved.

To which the man wired back:

Thanks for the advice. I'll start using it next week.

Back from Washington came this urgent message:

Regrettable decision involves uncertainties. Hydrochloric acid will produce sublimate invalidating reactions.

Which elicited this wire in reply:

Thanks again. Glad to know it's O.K.

This time there came the following urgent but clear message:

DON'T USE HYDROCHLORIC ACID!
IT WILL EAT HELL OUT OF YOUR TUBES!

Be clear! But how? It's easy to tell a writer he or she must be clear. No one can dispute the fact that it's excellent advice. The real question is: How do you achieve clarity? What makes one person's writing as clear as a plate glass window and another one's as murky as London fog?

You've heard people talk about the "gift of expression". Maybe some people get it as a gift, but most of us have to work for it. We've been working at it ourselves for forty years and hope to work at it for at least a few more. Sure, a certain amount of brainpower is a natural gift. Beyond that, however, it's a matter of applying brainpower to the art of communicating ideas.

If you want clarity, you're going to have to work for it. Sorry—we don't know any easy answer. You'll have to take your copy and sweat over it, using your God-given brains to figure out what should be changed and why. All we can do is give you some clues to help discover what's wrong. We can also assure you of this: When something isn't clear, there are definite reasons for the lack of clarity. Search and ye shall find. Communicating ideas is subject to logic the same as any other process.

One of the big problems in writing clearer copy is to spot vague, difficult, or fuzzy passages. It isn't always easy. The idea is so clear to you—you know what you're driving at to begin with—that you may not appreciate how difficult or confusing your message will be to someone else. You just can't react the way your reader will react.

That's why outside criticism is particularly helpful in the matter of clarity. It takes no great knowledge to tell you whether a piece of writing is perfectly clear and easy to understand. Your secretary can do it; so can anyone else in the office. They can give you a reader's opinion—and that's what you need. Fixing it up is your problem.

Whether you'll get an honest opinion—or just a flattering one—depends on you. If you take bad news gracefully—instead of showing irritation—and if you realize that it often takes several shots to hit a difficult target, you'll get real help. The ability to take criticism—and put it to good use—is fundamental to improving your writing. We've known some pretty fair writers who never realized their full potentialities because they never criticized themselves harshly enough. They were so delighted with anything they created they couldn't see the faults in it.

We have already covered two things which are vital to clarity—short, simple words and short, simply constructed sentences. What else is there? Another reason for vagueness, lack of clarity, or rambling is the lack of a clear, well-defined purpose in the mind of the writer. When you're analyzing a piece of writing that didn't come off exactly the way you wanted it to, ask yourself this question: What am I trying to accomplish with this? Think it over until you can state the purpose in *one simple sentence*.

When you have the purpose of the article or letter clearly in mind, take another look at it and ask a few more questions. Did I accomplish the purpose straightforwardly and directly, or did I beat around the bush? Did I put in extraneous material that isn't necessary? When you've clarified your own thinking, you may find a number of things that don't need to be there. You may also find a shorter, straighter path which leads directly to your goal.

Take a look at the following: 1,7,4,6,9,3,2,8,5,10.

What am I doing? Counting from 1 to 10. Perhaps you recognized it. It would be a lot easier to recognize, though, if I had done it in the usual, logical order, 1,2,3,4,5,6,7,8,9,10. The same thing is true of your writing. People will grasp the meaning a lot more easily if you present your ideas in the most logical, natural progression.

Logical organization is basic to clarity. The thoughts in a letter should proceed in logical sequence, one flowing into another from start to finish. The principle of logical organization applies to reports, articles, letters, paragraphs, sentences—even phrases. The ideas should run in a sequence which is easiest for the reader's mind to absorb. Let his or her mind work the easy way, not the hard way.

How do you achieve such a sequence? By thinking your letter out step-by-step before you write it—or before you do the second draft. The clarity of a letter is often improved by reversing the sequence of a couple of paragraphs. A paragraph may be made clearer by rejiggling the sequence of sentences; a sentence by changing the order of the phrases; a phrase by varying the order of words. Ideas should fit on top of one another like building blocks. Be sure you get the bottom blocks in first.

When you're writing a letter, memo, or release, try to state the purpose in one simple sentence. Don't start to write until you know exactly what you are trying to accomplish.

Having defined the purpose, what's the best way of achieving it? What facts and opinions must you present to accomplish that purpose? Which should logically come first? Which next?

Don't underestimate the importance of this idea. It's one of the ways a smart editor turns muddy copy into clear prose. When the meaning isn't immediately clear, he or she rearranges the order of the ideas to get a more logical flow of thought. When a letter, paragraph or sentence doesn't give a clear, sharp impression, you should do the same. Even little changes often make a big improvement in the ease of reading and understanding. Hard work? Yes, but you'll find the result tremendously gratifying. Clarity isn't an accident, it's the end product of good thinking.

Perhaps the problem has already been simplified to the question which shall we do, A or B. Well, what are the advantages and disadvantages of doing A? What are the advantages and disadvantages of doing B? Weighing advantages and disadvantages, which are the most important, and therefore which course of action is best?

In a report include only vital information, no hemming and hawing. Don't burden the reader with all the thoughts that occurred to you in reaching a decision, only the ones that were crucial. First write the body of your report, then the introduction. State the question simply, then your answer, and one or two of the most compelling reasons for your conclusions. Let the reader stop there if he wants to. Either that or go ahead and review the whole report. If your conclusion seems reasonable, that may be all that the people who asked for the report will be interested in.

Maybe you've heard the following rule for making a clear, forceful speech: Tell them what you are going to tell them, tell them, then tell them what you told them. There isn't always space to do this—nonetheless it's an important idea. The reader should be able to orient himself immediately when he starts to read your message, he ought to know exactly where he is at all points during the journey, and he ought to know where he stands when you're through with him. A message that has to be read in its entirety before the first part is clear needs to be reorganized.

While taking your reader on this journey, beware of sharp turns. You may know you are going to make a right angle turn in thought, but he or she doesn't. If you're not careful, you'll throw him right out of the car. Any time you change thought or direction in writing, put out your hand. Give him a signal so he'll know you are making a turn and in what direction. Keep him with you!

Sometimes an article or letter lacks clarity because it doesn't come to any definite conclusion. It leaves the reader up in the air. What is the reader supposed to do? Something or nothing? End your letters on a definite, positive note. When you have delivered the message, wrap it up. Either finish off the subject so that he knows nothing more is expected, or, if you want action, tell him what to do. Check your letters for this point. If you were the reader, would you know definitely, beyond doubt, what was expected of you? Or would you have to sit and figure it out? Wrap it up!

The ideas we've been talking about to improve clarity may seem like little things. They are. But that's what clarity comes from, attention to little things that help your message sink into the reader's mind with a minimum of effort on his part. Little as they seem, the fellow who masters them is on the way to being an excellent writer. Don't expect to do it in a day.

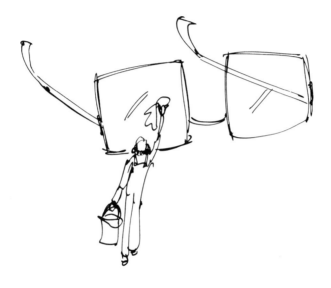

More About Clarity

"Vigorous writing is concise," says William Strunk. "A sentence should contain no unnecessary words, a paragraph no unnecessary sentences, for the same reason that a drawing should have no unnecessary lines and a machine no unnecessary parts."

Maybe you never thought of it that way. Words are cheap, so why not use all you want to? And back when you were learning to write, that may well have been the way to get a good mark from your teacher.

But that's not the way to get a good mark from the people you are now trying to communicate with. They are busy, interested in other things too, and not anxious to spend any more time than necessary on your message. If you get to the point and get it over with, they appreciate it. Your message, furthermore, will seem more clear and forceful.

Take a look at the following examples of excess verbiage culled from typical business letters.

1. Please feel free to write to us if you find yourself in need of more information.
    (Please write if you need more information.)

2. If at any time whatsoever we can be of additional service to you, kindly do not hesitate to let us know.
    (Whenever we can be of additional service, please let us know.)

3. We want to thank you very kindly again for your interest in Blank products.

    (Thank you again for your interest in Blank products.)

4. This is to express my personal thanks for your order.
    (Thank you for your order.)

5. Per your request, you will find enclosed is information on Blank valves.

    (Enclosed is the information you requested on Blank valves.)

6. May we ask that you kindly permit us to place your name on our mailing list?

    (May we place your name on our mailing list?)

7. In accordance with your recent inquiry at hand, we are pleased to be able to send you herewith a copy of our very latest catalog.

    (We are pleased to send you a copy of our latest catalog.)

8. This will acknowledge with thanks your letter of March 1, 1984, which is very much appreciated.

    (Your letter of March 1, 1984, is very much appreciated.)

9. We are anticipating being in the position of shipping your order soon.

    (We expect to ship your order soon.)

10. The undersigned wishes to acknowledge with deepest thanks receipt of your kind inquiry.

    (Thank you for your inquiry.)

Maybe these horrible examples don't apply to you. But the principle does. Examine the carbons of some of your recent business letters. Anyone who can't find ideas, words and phrases that ought to be eliminated is a rare exception.

Never set out to write a *long* letter, message, article or book. If you do, you're making a serious mistake at the very start. Instead, write a letter, message, article or book that is only as long as it has to be in order to be completely clear. If you stop there, you'll have done enough. Your readers will be grateful for your forbearance.

Excess wordage adds nothing. The secret of play writing, according to W. Somerset Maugham, can be given in two maxims: Stick to the point, and, whenever you can, cut. The same principles apply to good writing in any field.

Among the things to watch for are needless adverbs and adjectives. Every adjective and adverb changes the meaning of a sentence somewhat—or might change it as far as the reader knows. Every word adds an extra shade of meaning the reader must carry in his mind until he reaches the next period. Every adjective or adverb that isn't essential to the message you are trying to convey makes the reader's task just that more tedious and confusing.

Lots of adjectives repeat the meaning already obvious in the noun they modify. Either that or the shade of meaning they add is superfluous to the message. Why say "a round apple"? There aren't many square ones.

Adverbs often repeat meaning that is already obvious in the verb. For example, "He dashed hurriedly from the room." Have you ever seen anyone dash "unhurriedly"?

Or how about this: "The ravenously hungry man wolfed down a sandwich." Well, which is he, ravenous or hungry? Don't forget, we also picture him as "wolfing down" a sandwich. Many times, when we use two repetitive adjectives, either one would make a stronger impression than both of them together. Repetitive adjectives and adverbs make copy mushy and amateurish.

Good writers don't describe people with lots of adjectives. Instead they give you an impression by telling you the things people *do*, how they *act*, and how they appear to other people. They give specifics that reveal the character of the person, not just a string of descriptive adjectives. Instead of saying "He was a very large person," they report "He seemed to fill the doorway as he entered. Later, when he rose from his chair, the room was suddenly small and crowded."

If you stuff too many ideas into too short a space, too many descriptive adjectives, too many adverbs, too many qualifying phrases and clauses, most readers just browse along, getting the general sense if they can. But too much information is exactly that—too much. The picture gets foggy. It loses clarity and impact.

When you are looking for material that ought to be toned down or cut out pay special attention to superlatives and the word "very". Both are dead giveaways to the reader that you are trying too hard to impress him. Cut them both out and see if your copy doesn't sound more convincing. Nine out of ten times you'll notice an improvement. I have to cut out "very" more often than any other word in the dictionary. My runner-up is "really". Cutting down the use of these two words is "very" urgent and "really" important.

Your copy will be stronger and more convincing without them.

Another thing that makes writing mushy is the passive voice. A reader doesn't care to be told what happened to somebody. He'd much rather see it happen—so use the active voice whenever you can. Not "Jack was hit in the face by a grapefruit." Instead say: "Socko—the grapefruit hit Jack right in the face." With the active voice you can see it happen. The passive voice seems like a belated report describing something that happened quite a while ago. Don't say: "A new procedure was introduced." Instead report: "The management introduced a new procedure."

Examples and anecdotes, famous or otherwise, vastly improve the interest and clarity of the spoken or written word. Instead of talking in abstractions and generalities, why not illustrate what you are saying? Specific examples and anecdotes make your reasoning much easier to understand.

Suppose, for example, you want your readers to appreciate that some of America's most famous heroes were down-to-earth, unpretentious people. Well, why not tell them how George Washington, when he was elected President in 1789, refused to be addressed as "His Highness the President of the United States of America and Protector of the Rights of the Same?" Instead he suggested the legislators address him simply as "Mr. President". The title has continued to the present day.

Then tell your readers about the time, during Lincoln's term of office, that Senator Charles Sumner of Massachusetts called at The White House. It was early in the morning and he was amazed to find Lincoln polishing his boots. "Why do you polish your own boots, Mr. President?"

Lincoln continued to give one of the boots a vigorous brushing. "Whose boots did you think I polished?" he asked.

Where do you find stories like these? If you do much writing, you collect them all your life, in your head and in your files. You never know when you'll need a good story to make a point. And they are the most effective way to do it.

You can find useful anecdotes in the newspapers, magazines, and biographies in the library. I found the two I just used, about Washington and Lincoln, in a little booklet of patriotic stories The Economics Press published some years ago. It's out of print, but somebody inquired about it the other day and I dug out a copy just to recall what it looked like. Eureka! There they were—a dozen or so interesting little stories, just the kind you need to illustrate a point. What a find! I'd forgotten all about them!

Anecdotes and personal stories come in handy in all kinds of writing, you never know when. I startled myself recently by using one that must date all the way back to my childhood. I wrapped up a discussion of economic trends as follows:

> "The continuing Federal deficits are evidence, I'm afraid,
> that we, as a people, have been overreaching ourselves. It
> remind me of a parable I heard as a child about a dog
> crossing a bridge over a stream. He had a huge bone between
> his jaws. Suddenly, looking down into the water, he saw his
> own image. Thinking it was another dog with a bigger bone,
> he snapped at it and lost his own bone in the water. I can't

recall thinking of that story in fifty years, but there's something about the American people today that keeps bringing it to mind. What if, in snapping at a bigger bone, we lose the one we already have?"

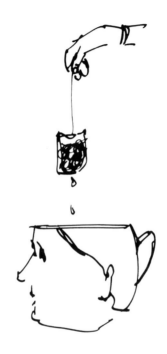

Soaking Time

When Karen G. got married, she resigned her job as a physical education instructor to devote full time to raising a family. Two years ago she decided the children were old enough so she could go back to work.

Instead of going back to teaching, Karen took some computer courses and got a job in the computer department of a steel company. It wasn't long, however, before her boss discovered that Karen had an unusual talent—the ability to express complicated ideas simply and clearly. So he asked her to edit the various reports he had to submit to other officers and departments. Others heard about her talent and asked her to edit their reports too.

How did she do it? Karen's method was surprisingly simple. First she took any compound or complex sentences that were the least bit difficult and broke them into two or more simple sentences. She arranged these in the most logical, easy-to-understand sequence. Next she crossed out any words that were not essential—such as adjectives or adverbs that made reading more complicated but added little or nothing to the meaning. Finally, she took out every complex or complicated-sounding word and substituted a more conversational one. That's all there was to Karen's formula, yet her editing attracted such attention that she soon moved on to an executive position with a firm of computer consultants.

We've already discussed every tool Karen used. There are, however, a few more which can be quite helpful. One of them I call soaking time.

When you write a letter or a report, you want it to be completely clear. The meaning should sink effortlessly into your reader's mind.

To achieve this, you have to make allowance for the way a reader's mind works. It is perfectly possible, for example, to present five thoughts in a row—each one of which is completely clear and in proper logical sequence—and still leave your reader befuddled. Why? Because you have presented the ideas too fast and furiously for his or her mind to absorb. You have tried to lay the next brick before the preceding one was securely in place.

The smarter the reader, the more rapidly he can absorb your ideas. Yet even the most alert and intelligent reader will get a clearer picture if each idea is firmly fixed in his mind before the next one is thrown at him. No matter how simple the ideas you present, they should not follow one another in too rapid sequence. It's important to allow a little soaking time for the idea to penetrate.

This is something that the skillful writer, consciously or unconsciously, learns to allow for. In dealing with a sequence of ideas, he or she will frequently repeat each one—slightly varied—before moving on. Sometimes all it takes is another phrase or sentence that amplifies the meaning. Either that or an example to clarify it. This repetition gives the reader a second chance to grab the brass ring securely before the merry-go-round spins on.

Take a look at the following examples. Each of them is clear. They can be understood. The underlined material we've added doesn't change the meaning a bit. But it does repeat the idea in a slightly different form, reinforce it, and give a little soaking time for the concept to become fixed in the reader's mind. The effect, we think, is greater clarity, particularly if the ideas are being presented as part of a logical sequence, each part of which must be understood before the next is clear.

Clear: The person who says he doesn't care whether his English is good or bad usually doesn't mean it. But the job of correcting his errors seems so hopelessly complicated that he has given up.

Clearer: The person who says he doesn't care whether his English is good or bad usually doesn't mean it. He'd like to use good English. But the job of correcting his errors seems so hopelessly complicated that he has given up. He isn't going to worry about it any longer.

See how the basic idea in each of the following paragraphs is repeated in the final sentence. The purpose is to nail the idea firmly in place before moving on.

Times change; so do job requirements. Your best guarantee of continued employment—as well as further advancement—is your ability to change with them. If you stay flexible—ready, willing and able to learn new things—you have nothing to fear from age or automation.

★　★　★

As your head comes above the surface, a slightly stronger push with your hands will hold it there long enough to inhale slowly through your mouth. Take your time inhaling: don't gulp.

★   ★   ★

Take a look at some of the repetition in the earlier parts of this chapter, repetition used to reinforce and strengthen an idea that has already been expressed.

When you write a letter or report, you want it to be completely clear. The meaning should sink effortlessly into your reader's mind.

★   ★   ★

Why? Because you have presented the ideas too fast and furiously for his mind to absorb. You have tried to lay the next brick before the preceding one was securely in place.

★   ★   ★

Take a look at the following examples. Each of them is clear. They can be understood.

★   ★   ★

The following excerpts are from a booklet about how to think. Note that the underlined sections do not introduce anything new. They don't change the meaning at all. Yet they do make it a lot easier to grasp, either by restating the same idea in different words or by giving an example.

Knowledge doesn't come from books—it comes from human observations and deductions. That's how it got in the books in the first place. The most

important knowledge we possess comes from ob-
serving and thinking, not from reading books or
listening to professors.

★　★　★

Creative thinkers consider not only sensible
answers but nonsensical ones too, hoping somewhere to find the germ of a new approach, a new
alternative that will produce a better answer. If an
idea doesn't work, they deliberately try the opposite.
If you can't think of a new way to cut grass, for
example, why not develop something that will keep
grass from growing so fast?

★　★　★

Try to visualize each proposed solution. How
would it work in actual practice? Try to create a
mental picture of your plan in operation. How would
people have to act in order for your proposed solution to work? Can you visualize people acting this
way? Does the picture seem realistic—or partly
wishful thinking?

★　★　★

A skillful writer often repeats the same idea quickly in
two or three different ways. If the idea is especially important, he or she may give more than one example to illustrate
it. Experienced writers do this to achieve force and clarity.
The average person often does the same thing in conversation, saying something several different ways to be sure it
is clear. If you want your writing to be forceful and easy to
understand, do the same thing when you write. Your reader
won't be tired by the repetition. He'll appreciate it. After all,

55

you're making his job easier.

Whenever you run across a piece of writing that is unusually clear and interesting, look back and see if you can figure out how the writer achieved that effect. In most cases you'll find a lot of quick, short repetition, the writer saying the same thing in a number of ways, quoting others who agree with his thinking, and giving examples that illustrate what he is talking about.

Comparisons add interest and clarity. So do examples, "for instances". In the last page or so we've made comparisons with laying bricks, grabbing a brass ring on the merry-go-round, letting something soak in, and nailing something in place. Each has been used to clarify and drive home the meaning of an important point. You can use them the same way. When an idea isn't as clear as you'd like, figure out something that will help the reader grasp your meaning.

And be sure you don't present ideas faster than the normal human mind can absorb them. A teacher of social studies, for example, started an essay on economic democracy as follows:

"Democracy is a hallowed word in our society. Its very name denotes free choice, relief from oppression, self-determination, civil liberties, and rights of expression."

WHOA! STOP RIGHT THERE—YOU'VE LOST ME. What are the five things democracy denotes? Without looking back, can you recall all five of them? We couldn't.

The writer presents too many concepts too fast for the human mind—at least our kind of mind—to appreciate. If the ideas are worth mentioning, shouldn't they be put forward with a little more detail so the reader can savor and appreciate each one?

People need time to absorb ideas—even those expressed in language they're familiar with. It makes copy more understandable to eliminate longer words, less familiar words, and difficult sentence constructions. What's even more important, however, is to repeat ideas with small talk spaced in between. It gives the reader more than one chance to get what you're driving at.

A Word About Letters

Why don't people write better letters and reports? The biggest stumbling block, believe it or not, isn't a matter of technique or writing ability. It's a matter of mental attitude. The reason most people don't write better is because they are too self-centered. Self-centeredness is the curse of good writing. This doesn't apply, of course, to you or me. Neither of us is self-centered. But it does apply to an amazing number of other people.

In writing of any kind the important thing is to plant an idea in the reader's mind or to stimulate his feelings or emotions. In all good writing, one person and only one person is important—the reader. Yet what happens when the average person sits down to write a letter or report? Somewhere in his conscious or unconscious mind an insidious thought raises its head: *What will the reader think of me?* The more that thought interferes with concentrating on the reader, the poorer his or her writing becomes.

Why do so many executives, lawyers, scientists, and engineers sound like executives, lawyers, scientists, and engineers in everything they write? Because that's what they're trying to sound like—they wouldn't want people to think of them in any other way. They're more concerned with the impression they're making than they are about the message.

And what happens when an executive comes along who isn't trying to impress anybody, who's just trying to get his or her ideas across in the simplest, clearest fashion to the reader or listener? More often than not he or she is outstanding! He impresses far more than those who are striving to be impressive.

Perhaps you work for the largest, most powerful organization in the world. If so, when you start to write or dictate, forget it! Your corporation consists of pleasant, friendly people. So get politely to the point, wrap it up, and wish your correspondent well. Write to him or her in the same language you would use if you were carrying on a conversation across the desk. "Stay loose!" as my old baseball coach used to say.

Maybe you're an exception—self-centeredness doesn't affect your writing. But don't bet on it. We'd lay odds of ten to one that it occasionally hurts the effectiveness of your letters the same as it does ours. If you'd like to know more about yourself, get out some old letters or reports—ones you wrote at least six months to a year ago so they are no longer fresh in your mind. Give them a cold, dispassionate once-over. See what you think of the person who wrote them. Was he or she working solely for the reader, or did he occasionally strain a bit to make an impression? Does he sound direct, friendly, and unassuming, or does he let a touch of conceit creep in every now and then? You'd be amazed at what you can learn about yourself from old letters—things you've never been conscious of before. Don't just think about this—do it! Get out some old letters and take a look.

By the way, how do you start your letters? Dear Mr. Jones? Dear Miss Smith? That's all right—nobody would think of criticizing you for it. But there *is* a better way to get into your subject. After all, if Mr. Jones or Miss Smith were sitting across the desk from you, would you say "Dear"? Not without blushing a bit, probably.

So why not start your letter just the way you would talk if they were sitting there listening? Start your letter with a conversational salutation that uses the person's name just the way you would in speaking to them. Try these salutations, for example:

Thank you, Mr. Smith!

Your order for 25 cases of lubricating oil arrived this morning.

No, Miss Jones—

we haven't forgotten you! Your request for . . .

Yes, Mr. Brown,

we can reserve a fine room for you July 17.

We're delighted, Ms. Howe,

that you've chosen us to handle the arrangements for your party.

Say, George,

whatever became of that order you were going to place with us?

You're right, Mr. Kinnard!

We did make a mistake on your last order.

It's a pleasure, Miss Keith,

to add your name to our mailing list.

We've missed you, Mr. Karl!

You haven't placed an order with us since June 1.

Last time I saw you, Mr. Pennington,

you were talking about the possibility of . . .

I've used salutations like these on most of my letters for the last thirty years without a single complaint. And the method does have a tremendous advantage—it doesn't waste any time whatsoever on pontificating or introductory remarks. As the writer, it gets you right into the middle of the subject. All you have to do is go on from there. It makes your letters sound pointed and dynamic, and with no beating around the bush.

Try it! But don't write a letter to "Dear Mr. Jones" then change the salutation. Start out by saying:

Your proposal, Mr. Jones,

is very interesting.

Then write the rest of the letter.

When you start out this way, you'll find yourself getting right down to brass tacks. Your letter will be clearer and more forceful than the one you would have written to "Dear Mr. Jones".

Starting a sales letter is different. The first thing you *must* do, one way or another is get the reader interested. If he doesn't get interested right away, he won't bother to read the rest of your letter.

There's an old device known to fiction writers and story-tellers as "the narrative hook". You'll find it in almost every short story or novel you read. In fact, if you don't find it, you may drop the story right there and turn to something else.

The narrative hook is an opening incident or situation that so mystifies, intrigues, or interests the reader that he or she wants to keep on reading in order to find out how it turns out. The fiction writer works hard on this narrative hook because his success depends on keeping the reader with him. It's just as important to a letter writer too.

In some cases, when the reader has already inquired, or you know that he is already interested in a subject, gaining and keeping his interest is no great problem. All you have to do is to identify clearly and immediately the subject you are writing about.

An unsolicited sales letter, however, or a letter opening a brand new subject not of obvious interest to the recipient, is a horse of a different color. A letter of this kind *must* have a narrative hook. It must talk *immediately* about some situation so interesting or vital to the reader that he or she is eager to continue reading. Otherwise your letter is apt to join that portion of the day's mail that is consigned, unread, to the wastebasket.

The minute the recipient glances at your introductory remarks, your letter is involved in a life-or-death struggle. If it wins his interest, your message may get across. If not, it hasn't a chance.

This is obviously no time to engage, as so many writers do, in general introductory remarks, or in talk about their company and its fine reputation. You have ten seconds, or less, to say something vital, something that assures that the reader will continue reading. What is it? You'll have to figure that out for yourself; if you can't, you'll never be a persuasive letter writer. All we can tell you is that it must be something that excites interest—usually something about *the reader*, rarely, if ever, something about *you* or *your company*.

One of the gratifying things about sales letters is that they are one form of writing about which there can be no argument. If you want to decide which of two sales letters is the better, just mail them both out at the same time under identical circumstances. The one that brings in more orders is the better letter.

Direct mail is a specialty. People write books about it and make a career of it. I've been in it thirty odd years myself, selling employee training materials to business and industry. This is a book about all kinds of expository writing, however, and I'm not going to dig deeply into direct mail. Suffice it to pass along a few observations, some of which may not jibe exactly with the generally accepted notions.

1. Conversational language is vital. Simplicity pays, not pretense.

2. Citing the benefits of your product is not always the best way to get attention. An interesting anecdote, especially one that touches off kindly emotions, may be much better. After you've got the prospect's attention, and put him or her in a pleasant mood, then talk about your product.

3. Be honest. You can be optimistic in a sales letter, but don't make statements you don't believe. If you don't believe something, don't say it, because most pros-

pects won't believe it either. They'll begin to distrust you.

As a matter of interest I'm including here three of the most successful sales letters we've circulated. Their success isn't a matter of personal opinion—the orders from each are still tumbling out of mail sacks.

A Sad Letter - With A Happy Ending!

Here's a letter we received from a man canceling his subscription to our little magazine, BITS & PIECES. It's genuine--I think you'll recognize it as the real thing:

*I have enjoyed your BITS & PIECES ever since
I first subscribed to it. I wish I had known
of it 25 years ago--I'd have acquired a lot
of sound advice at a time when it was needed
most.*

*Not renewing my subscription to it is like
parting company with a friend you don't expect to meet again. I do not like to tell
you I am not renewing. I wish I could afford
it, but at today's cost of living for a retiree--
I can't.*

L. Viall

We wrote Mr. Viall to tell him we were extending his subscription anyway, and asked permission to quote his letter to show how subscribers <u>feel</u>

about this magazine. They get emotionally attached to it--cherish it like an old and close friend.

BITS & PIECES fans don't just read the magazine--they wear it out. It's the kind of thing you can read today, then pick up two weeks later and browse through again. It leaves you with a warm and pleasant feeling every time.

Underneath its pleasant exterior, BITS & PIECES has a serious mission. One purpose is to enable you to recognize and acknowledge the importance in your organization of the people who handle people--from company president right down to the newest foreman. Their skill, or lack of it, determines the tone and character of your entire operation.

The second purpose is to enable you to pass along to these people some practical tips, inspiration, and insight into human nature. People need this kind of guidance far more than they realize or care to admit.

It takes time to make a good executive, supervisor, or foreman, and experience is the greatest teacher. But it also helps to have a little coaching along the way. That's why we created BITS & PIECES.

One of the secrets of BITS & PIECES is our editor, a pleasant chap with some gray in his hair, a twinkle in his eye, and his tongue in his cheek. Perhaps we should also mention the world of experience under his belt.

He's the kind of fellow you love to have a chat with. And that's exactly the way you feel

when you read each monthly issue. One of our subscribers says he can usually tell when the magazine has arrived--he can hear the people in the
mail room laughing.

BITS & PIECES is completely unpretentious,
obviously written by and for real, down-to-earth
human beings. Most of the contents are just
plain common sense. Effective leadership is
mostly common sense--even though it takes time,
experience, and a lot of guidance to develop.

Best of all, BITS & PIECES is quick and
easy to read. You'll find items to make you
chuckle...others to make you think. That's a
wonderful combination to open people's minds...
to make them think about doing things a little
differently and a little better.

Try this publication for all your executives, supervisors and managers. They will
enjoy it. Just send in the enclosed card and
we'll start your service with the next issue.

Sincerely,

I WISH YOU COULD MEET HELEN. . . .

     She's the woman who writes YOUR TELEPHONE
PERSONALITY, our special training program to
improve the way people handle the telephone.
She's so warm, perceptive, and pleasant, you
couldn't help but be favorably impressed.

     Helen won her spurs the hard way. She
came to us as a general office worker, but she
was so pleasant, and handled people so well,
that we asked her to serve as a receptionist.
She also had a lovely voice, so we gave her
the telephone, too.

     It was almost unbelievable, the impres-
sion Helen made on our customers. Two or
three times a month one customer or another
would insist on speaking with our President or
General Manager just to put in a word for
Helen and say how beautifully she had handled
their calls. Eventually I asked Helen: "Do
you think you could put down on paper some of
the ideas and principles you use in answering
the phone?"

     "I'll be delighted to try," she said.

That was the start of YOUR TELEPHONE PER-
SONALITY. Now, only a few years later, more than
50,000 people get a new issue every two weeks--
more of Helen's warm, workable ideas for making
friends and giving excellent service by telephone.
It's a sincere, genuine publication, straight
from Helen's mind and heart. She signs every
issue "Affectionately, Helen" and that's exactly
what she means.

YOUR TELEPHONE PERSONALITY is for operators,
secretaries and all those who handle inquiries,
complaints, orders and other business calls. Its
purpose is to make sure every one of these calls
is recognized as an important image-building
opportunity for your company.

The publication is pleasant, personal and
professional. Written as one operator talking to
others who handle telephone calls, sharing her
enthusiasm for a job she believes is tremendously
important, showing how to give every caller a
good impression of your company.

Today large sums are invested on advertising,
public relations and in training sales and service
personnel. Yet a great deal of important business
is transacted by phone. Doesn't it make equally
good sense to give those who handle your calls
some training in the art of dealing with people?

If just a few of the ideas in YOUR TELEPHONE
PERSONALITY rub off on the people in your firm...
and we're sure they will...you'll have the small
cost back many times over. Its suggestions will
be helpful to anyone who handles incoming calls
at any point, especially customer inquiries or
complaints.

Try the service and see for yourself. Just give me permission on the enclosed card to send copies of YOUR TELEPHONE PERSONALITY for the people you want to have them.

If they're not enthusiastic...and if you're unhappy with the series for any reason...just write me and ask for a refund of the unused portion of your subscription. We'll send a check immediately.

Sincerely,

She was so good I almost didn't hire her.

"You're too well-educated," I said. "You're over-qualified." Her name was Pam and she was an Oxford graduate, just over from England.

"But Mr. Beckley," she protested with her correct British accent, "I need the job. Please give me a chance." I did, and The Economics Press was never the same again.

Pam was a model secretary and office worker--extremely intelligent, punctual, almost never absent, diligent, hardworking. And Pam hardly ever made mistakes, something of a rarity even in those days. Furthermore, Pam had the capacity to <u>enjoy</u>

her work. She relished tackling a job and getting
it done. And she was very popular. The other
office workers found her understanding and helpful; they liked her sense of humor too.

Pam's one fault, if you can call it that, was
that she had an overabundance of initiative. She
was always saying, "Mr. Beckley, why don't we do
it this way?" It was hard to keep up with her.

One day Pam came to me with one of her bright
ideas. "Why don't we put out a publication for
office workers?" she said. At that time we published biweekly bulletins for improving the perfor-
mance of managers, supervisors and salespeople.
Pam pointed out that office personnel needed help
as much as anyone.

And so Pam the secretary became Pam the writer.
She thought up the topics--such as how to avoid
mistakes or impress customers--and she wrote the
copy. I did the editing, and we called the result
PAM SAYS. She's still writing the issues every
two weeks, but we've changed the title to OFFICE
TOPICS--to reflect the fact that more and more
males are now doing clerical work.

Pam's no longer my secretary, but because she once
was, a lot of other secretaries and clerks are
better at their jobs today. Pam got married (her
last name is now Abas) and moved out to Idaho.
Today she directs little theater, and you may
have seen her as the Mother Superior in Clint
Eastwood's movie, Bronco Billy.

You may have a "Pam" working for you. If so, you
probably wish all your office employees were more
like her. Well, they can be; you can help them

move in that direction.

I invite you to subscribe to OFFICE TOPICS for
each member of your office team--clerks, secretaries, receptionists and the like--and see the results for yourself.

Our Special Offer

Give OFFICE TOPICS a try; distribute it to everyone who could benefit from it every two weeks. If
at any time you're dissatisfied with the service,
for _any_ reason, you may terminate it just by telling us to stop. Request a refund, and we'll send
you the unused balance of your subscription immediately. Fair enough?

It would be a pleasure to serve you!

Sincerely,

Cut! Cut! Cut!

Americans worship wordiness.

A child is praised by his parents when he or she says his first word. The same when he learns to read or write. Words are wonderful!

In school the emphasis is on quantity. The assignment is a 250 word composition or 500 word essay. The child searches diligently for enough wordy ways of expressing ideas to meet the requirement. Rewards for clarity and conciseness are not mentioned.

The same, in a way, is true even of professional writing. Free-lance writers are often paid by the word or the inch. Charles Dickens wrote some of his famous novels as serials at so much a word. That's undoubtedly why the main plots slow down every once in a while and duck into this side alley or that one. Charles was busy picking up a few more pence. He was not in the least hurry to get the story over with.

And show me a professional writer who isn't prouder of a long article under his by-line than a short one. There's no such animal!

Yet there is also an obvious need in this world for writing that is clear and forceful, that conveys meaning and intent with a minimum waste of time and effort. We need more of that kind of writing in our business and personal letters, reports, notices, memoranda, instruction sheets, textbooks, articles, and yes, even novels.

Nobody seems to appreciate this more than experienced, professional writers themselves. Whenever famous authors give advice about writing, the thing they most commonly emphasize is simplicity of expression, eliminating unnecessary words, phrases, and sentences. Dr. Samuel Johnson recommended: "Read over your compositions, and when you meet with a passage which you think is particularly fine, strike it out." In other words, don't fall so much in love with anything you've written that you lose your objectivity.

This is more of a problem than most people realize. If you start out with the assumption that most of the things you write are already pretty good, you're not going to improve much. It reminds me of my old friend Percy who was a very intelligent person with a good command of words. But he fell in love with everything he wrote. He simply couldn't pick up a piece of writing he had done and see that it had some serious flaws. He never seemed to improve beyond a certain point. If you already think you're wonderful, what incentive is there?

Whenever you're in doubt whether something should stay in your copy or come out, cut it! You can always put it back later if you want to. Most of the time, you'll find things are better without it. Your message is cleaner, clearer, and more forceful.

Sometimes not merely words, phrases or sentences should be cut, but complete paragraphs. Why? Not necessarily because they are poorly written. Sometimes they introduce a different viewpoint at the wrong moment, just when it interferes with another, more important point you are trying to make.

Consider, for example, the following item which was

submitted for BITS & PIECES, a pocket-sized, 24-page magazine for executives. The magazine consists of very brief anecdotes and articles about handling people, inspirational items, and a little humor. Here's how it was submitted:

Senator Patrick Leahy of Vermont is not a gambling man. Returning from a speaking engagement in Las Vegas recently, he met Senator Charles Mathias of Maryland in the airport. While they were waiting for their flight back to Washington, Senator Mathias asked Leahy whether he had played the slot machines during his visit.

When Senator Leahy told him he hadn't, Senator Mathias persuaded him to put a quarter into one of the airport slot machines. Immediately the bells went off and $50 in quarters poured out of the machine.

A few minutes later, his pockets bulging with quarters, Senator Leahy set off an airport metal detector. When security personnel told him to put his pocket change in a plastic tray, the senator filled nine trays with the coins.

In the boarding lounge, the senator was explaining what had happened to some other waiting passengers. To illustrate, he put a coin in a nearby nickel slot machine, pulled the lever—and $20 worth of nickels poured out.

With that kind of luck, friends say, Senator Leahy ought to consider running for President.

We ran the item in the magazine as follows. See if you notice any difference:

Senator Patrick Leahy of Vermont is not a gambling man. Returning from a speaking engagement in Las Vegas recently, he met Senator Charles Mathias of Maryland in the airport. While they were waiting for their flight back to Washington, Senator Mathias asked Leahy whether he had played the slot machines during his visit.

When Senator Leahy told him he hadn't, Senator Mathias persuaded him to put a quarter into one of the airport slot machines. Immediately the bells went off and $50 in quarters poured out of the machine.

In the boarding lounge, the senator was explaining what had happened to some other waiting passengers. To illustrate, he put a coin in a nearby nickel slot machine, pulled the lever—and $20 worth of nickels poured out.

With that kind of luck, friends say, Senator Leahy ought to consider running for President.

All we did was eliminate the third paragraph. Nothing else. Why? Because the point of the anecdote is that Senator Leahy was unbelievably lucky. The delay in getting through the turnstile had nothing to do with that. It simply diverts attention from the main point. So we knocked it out. If this were a news item, it ought to be left in, but not in BITS & PIECES. We need and use every inch of space we have for other purposes.

Ha! Ha!, Ho! Ho!

A little humor is a big help when you're trying to make a point. Used inexpertly, however, it's a dangerous thing. It can ruin what would otherwise have been a good speech, good article or good chapter.

Some things, I guess, are funny to everyone. But who knows, for sure, what they are? Before I use a humorous story in any of our publications I always check it with a number of people first. If any of them are the least bit un-enthusiastic, out it goes! I rarely take a chance on it.

Dick Borden had some excellent rules for using humor in a speech. They apply equally well to humor in writing. Don't use a humorous story just to be funny. Don't use it unless it illustrates the point you are talking about. And don't tell it as if you thought you were telling a funny story. Tell it in a very casual way just as you would tell any other anecdote. When you reach the point, if the audience bursts out laughing, pause a moment until you have their attention again, then continue.

But don't pause as if you expected people to laugh. Because, if they don't, you'll be standing there with egg on your face. Just keep right on going, as though you had no intention of trying to be funny in the first place, and show how the story illustrates the point you were talking about. Do the same thing when you are writing. Don't let the reader suspect you hoped he would be doubled over with laughter.

A great many people, including a fair number of professional writers, take too long to tell a supposedly funny story. They throw in too many details that are unessential to the point. When someone starts to tell a story that I suspect is supposed to be a joke, I sit there impatiently waiting for the point. When they try to hold my attention with extraneous details or unnecessary repetition, I writhe in my seat. A funny story is always funnier if you set up the picture in fewer words and get to the point faster.

In judging humor over the years, I lean strongly toward what I would call "realistic" humor. The humorous situation is a true story, or so close to a real life situation that it could easily have happened just the way it is told. Make-believe humor leaves me cold—humor that doesn't ring true to life and is obviously manufactured out of whole cloth just to try to get a laugh.

Take the following story, for example, which appeared as a filler in a little magazine for salespeople. The main content of the magazine is short articles intended to inspire, train, and amuse salespeople.

> A farmer, driving back from the market in his truck, pulled over to the side when he saw a disabled truck on the shoulder of the road. The other truck was full of penguins, and the driver was worried; he had promised to deliver the penguins to the city zoo before three o'clock.
>
> "Can I help you?" the farmer asked.
>
> "Yeah," the truck driver said, "you sure can. Will you send out someone from a garage to fix my truck, and take these penguins to the zoo for me?"
>
> "Well," the farmer said, "I'll be glad to call a garage, but I'm on my way home, and the zoo is quite a bit out of my way."

"Look," the driver said. "This is important. I'll give you $100 to take these penguins to the zoo."

"Well, all right," the farmer said. The two men loaded the penguins into the farmer's truck, and he drove off.

An hour later, a mechanic from the local garage had fixed the truck, and the driver decided to go to the zoo and see that the penguins had arrived safely. As he drove up to the entrance to the zoo, he saw the farmer's truck, with the penguins still on board, leaving the zoo. The truck driver made a U-turn and caught up to the farmer, who pulled over to the side of the road. The truck driver stopped and walked up to the farmer's truck. "What's the idea?" he said. "I asked you to take these penguins to the zoo."

"Well," the farmer said, "I did. But I had $40 left over from the money you gave me, so I thought I'd take them to a movie too."

This story lets me down. It never happened, never will, and was manufactured expressly to try to be funny. And it isn't very funny. If I were a sales manager, buying this little magazine to inspire and train my salespeople, I'd be disappointed at this flagrant waste of space. A brief poor joke is bad enough, a long one is hard to forgive.

Here's another story from the same magazine:

When aluminum combination windows were first introduced on the market, Jack de Courcy was employed as a door-to-door canvasser. His job was to knock on every door to try to get appointments to demonstrate the product to homeowners. Jack worked with another salesman named Emerson, a "closer" who would go to the appointments with Jack to try to close the sale. The appointments were usually *scheduled for the evening, so they could demonstrate the model window and explain its features to both the husband and the wife.*

One evening the two men had an appointment with a couple in Wadington, a small town in upstate New York. The presentation went well, and the couple signed a contract for 15 windows and a door. Jack and Emerson had said goodnight and gone back to their car when Emerson remembered that they hadn't measured the kitchen window. Rather than go back into the house and perhaps upset the sale, Emerson decided to get the measurements from the outside.

With the help of a flashlight, they made their way to the back of the house, and Emerson climbed up on a garbage can and measured the window. He had just finished when the woman of the house entered the kitchen and was startled to see him standing outside her kitchen window. There was little Emerson could do but smile and tip his hat, then the two men beat a hasty retreat.

Two weeks later, Jack and Emerson were working in the nearby village of Ogdensburg, which is best known for its large state mental hospital. When the installers arrived in Wadington to put in the windows, the woman asked them where Emerson was. "Oh," the driver told her, "he's in Ogdensburg."

The woman nodded. "You know," she said, "I thought there was something wrong with that man."

This story is different. It really happened, or might well have happened. I doubt if anyone would dream up anything like this. It is also about salesmen, therefore of greater interest to salesmen. And even though the point brings no uproarious laughter, it *is* surprising and amusing.

I have one suggestion. The story could easily be re-written, eliminating three sentences in the first two paragraphs, and be just as effective. Take a look at this and see if you think we've lost anything.

When aluminum combination windows were first intro-duced on the market, Jack de Courcy was employed as a door-to-door canvasser. Jack worked with another salesman named Emerson, a "closer" who would go to the appoint-ments with Jack to try to close the sale.

One evening the two men had an appointment with a couple in Wadington, a small town in upstate New York. The presentation went well, and the couple signed a contract for 15 windows and a door. Jack and Emerson had said good-night and gone back to their car when Emerson remembered that they hadn't measured the kitchen window.

With the help of a flashlight, they made their way to the back of the house, and Emerson climbed up on a garbage can and measured the window. He had just finished when the woman of the house entered the kitchen and was startled to see him standing outside her kitchen window. There was little Emerson could do but smile and tip his hat, then the two men beat a hasty retreat.

Two weeks later, Jack and Emerson were working in the nearby village of Ogdensburg, which is best known for its large state mental hospital. When the installers arrived in Wadington to put in the windows, the woman asked them where Emerson was. "Oh," the driver told her, "he's in Ogdensburg."

The woman nodded. "You know," she said, "I thought there was something wrong with that man."

Why bother with such minor changes? Because it makes

the reader's job easier, and the story comes to the point a little faster. Would you like to improve your writing a lot? If so, you'll have to accept the fact that little improvements are worthwhile. A lot is usually an accumulation of little bits. Eventually small improvements here and there add up to something really noticeable.

THE ROAD
TO EXCELLENCE.

Potpourri

So far I've been trying to do exactly what the title of this book promised, to give you "SOME IDEAS TO IMPROVE YOUR WRITING". I've already told you the most important things I know about the subject. Next, I intend to show you how these ideas can be applied in specific instances, and, hopefully, to convince you that they are well worth using.

First, however, let's look in the corners and sweep up a few miscellaneous tidbits I hate to let go unmentioned.

First, my favorite book about writing, PUBLIC SPEAKING AS LISTENERS LIKE IT by Richard Borden. Sure, the title says public speaking, but don't let that fool you. Borden presents a four-point formula that is vital to anyone who is trying to get *listeners or readers* interested in what he has to say and keep them interested. I must have discovered the book almost 30 years ago. The formula, which has helped my writing ever since, was (1) HO HUM! (2) WHY BRING THAT UP? (3) FOR INSTANCE (4) SO WHAT?

In the first place, says Borden, you have to assume that your listener (reader) has heard dozens of boring speeches. "Ho hum," he is sitting there thinking, "this will be another one."

That being the case, your first sentence must be so interesting or startling that it makes him sit bolt upright. Like the minister who started his summer sermon: "It's goddamned hot in here." After a pause he raised his finger in solemn reproof and said: "That's what I heard a man say as I walked in here this afternoon."

Why bring that up? Okay, says the listener or reader, you've got my attention. But why bring that up? So tell him how it relates to the subject you intend to discuss and why. You mentioned the profanity because you think it's a bad habit and you'll be glad to tell him the reasons why.

As you present your main points, start giving "for instances" to illustrate each, sometimes more than one for instance. Anecdotes, historical incidents, personal experiences.

When you run out of for instances, wind it up. Don't ruin your speech or article by repeating generalities. Your audience is wondering: "So what?" So reach a conclusion. Tell them what to do, how to vote, what to eat to stay healthy, how to contribute—some action you expect as a result of this message.

Borden's book was published by Harper & Bros. in 1935. Unfortunately, it's finally out of print. I've never read anything more pointed and practical.

I visited the library the other day to see if there were any helpful ideas about grammar, spelling or punctuation that I could pass along. When I saw the shelves loaded with books on English grammar, style, and usage, it shook my confidence. How could I have been a writer and publisher for more than thirty years without paying more attention to these scholarly dissertations? Was I cheating? How long would it be before the authorities caught up with me?

Perhaps that, in itself, is the most important message I have to give you in this area: don't be intimidated. There are no "laws" of grammar or punctuation—much to the disappointment of people who make a fetish of such things.

There are, instead, simply customary ways of using words and punctuation marks that are observed by most people with a reasonable amount of education. If you want to do or say something differently, you're perfectly free to do it. No one can stop you. If enough people do it, the usage changes. The so-called "law" is repealed.

A typical example is the expression which was popular a few years ago, "I couldn't care less." Nowadays that's been shortened by many people to "I could care less." What the speaker still means, whether he says it or not, is that he *couldn't* care less. Nevertheless, the way of expressing that idea has changed.

If you associate with reasonably well-educated people, correct grammar comes naturally. It's the way you've learned to talk because that's the way you heard other people talk. If you pick up a grammar book and look at a number of "rules", you'll find that you observe most of them even though you've never heard of them before. You don't have to memorize all those rules because they describe the usual way you've learned to speak.

So cheer up! If you're afraid of your grammar, don't worry about it. Just write naturally, the way you talk. And, if it's important, have your secretary or a friend, someone who is familiar with good grammar, check it for you. Learn a little from each experience. Ask what was wrong in each case and try to remember it next time.

If you're really worried about it, get the smallest, simplest book about grammar you can find in the library. Avoid the thick, lengthy tomes. Put it next to the chair in which you watch television. When the program is boring, turn the TV off and pick up the grammar. Don't try to memorize anything. Just look through it and read anything that looks interesting. Believe it or not, you'll find it a lot easier to read and the contents more practical than you did in the 5th grade. If something bores you, skip ahead. You already do most of the things it recommends, even though you may not be conscious of it.

When you're through with that, put the dictionary next to your chair. Most dictionaries have excellent sections about the use of punctuation. Some also have advice about spelling. The reading really isn't dull—not compared to most television—especially if you realize the subject is important to you. In a night or two, at most three or four, you'll have a more practical knowledge of both subjects. You'll also know where to look when you have a problem.

Just follow the rules you know, and don't worry too much about minor infractions. But don't reach out for strange words you're not sure of—either the meaning or the spelling. Check the dictionary first.

Perhaps you've noticed one of my "mistakes" in punctuation. The general practice is that when a sentence ends with quotation marks, the final punctuation—usually a period or question mark—is put *inside* the quotation marks. For example:

Tom replied curtly, "I'm going home."

I have no argument with this custom when, as in the above example, the period also applies to the material inside the quotation marks. When it doesn't, I object. For example:

The name of the movie was "Gone with the Wind."

This placement of the period doesn't make sense to me. The period applies to the whole sentence. It doesn't apply to the material inside the quotation marks. Therefore, I prefer:

The name of the movie was "Gone with the Wind".

So that's the way I do it. I get occasional letters of complaint from dedicated grammarians. I always enjoy telling them that as a writer, I help create new usage, not simply follow the old.

Obviously, there's a lot more that could be said on this subject, but I don't want to hold up the many, many readers who already know all these technicalities. I'll wrap up the subject by mentioning what I call "The Big Bloopers". These are mistakes most people recognize immediately and tend to think: "Oh, oh! He or she isn't very well educated."

One of these bloopers is the word "ain't". It's a wonderful word, the only contraction available for "am not". Nevertheless, it's a no-no. The prestigious grammarians beat us practical people to the punch years ago and persuaded everyone to think it was poor English. So—like it or not—you'd better accept that fact.

Another blooper is the use of "don't" when the proper word is "doesn't". Never say "He don't", "She don't", or "The faucet don't work". The proper word is "doesn't" and almost everyone knows it. If you didn't know it, you do now.

Another one that sets off an alarm is use of the word "was" instead of "were" in a clause that starts with "if". If the clause states something that clearly isn't so—you're just imagining it—always use *were* not *was*. For example:

If I were the boss, I'd fire him.

(You're *not* the boss so use *were* instead of *was*.)

If he were the boss, he'd fire me.

(He's *not* the boss, either, so use *were* instead of *was*.)

On the other hand, if the proposition in the "if" clause might be either true or false, use the word you would normally use.

If he *was* right, I am wrong. If I *was* right, he's wrong.

Nobody knows who's right. The "if" clause isn't obviously false in either case, so don't use "were".

"If I was" and "If he was" are *usually* wrong. Whenever you hear them, or are about to use them, take another look. If the "if" clause is untrue, purely imaginative, use *were* instead.

When you are explaining a proposition or a general rule that is subject to a number of exceptions, always state the rule first. Give the reader something to measure the exceptions against. Otherwise he is helpless to understand or judge them until he reaches the end of the sentence.

Don't, for example, write something like this:

If you supply proof of citizenship, if you have been a member of this community for five years, if you have been interviewed favorably by the president of the council, and if you accompany your application with a certified check for $100, we'd be glad to consider your request.

Instead say:

We'd be glad to consider your request subject to the following conditions:

1. You supply a proof of citizenship.
2. You have been a member of the community for five years.

Etc.

Lawyers are very prone to a series of if this, if that, if the other thing, before they get to the point. So are public notices.

Steer clear of using the "latter" and the "former". They just make life more complicated, two more things your reader has to remember.

For example:

The Smiths had two children, Sam and Jack. The latter studied medicine; the former became a lawyer.

Now, which one was the doctor and which one the lawyer?

It would have been simpler to remember if the writer had said:

The Smiths had two children, Sam and Jack. Jack studied medicine, Sam became a lawyer.

Why introduce two additional concepts, the latter and the former? They don't do a bit of good, simply complicate the situation.

The more you get people and conversations into your copy, the more readily people will read it. When you don't have actual quotations, try substitutes like these:

He as much as said: "Look, Mr. B. . . . . . . "

The conversation probably went something like this: "What are you doing over there, Charlie?" "None of your business. Why are you so curious?"

It was easy to imagine one of them saying: "This is a cinch! Take your time." And the other one replying: ". . . . ."

Rudolph Flesch has pointed out that this is an important difference he has noticed between amateur and professional writers. Professionals go to any length to get in some conversation even if they have to imagine it. Amateurs tend to shy away, even from quotes of a few words.

One final word of advice: When you have to edit your own copy, cool it first. Wait until the topic is no longer hot in your mind—at least until the next day if possible. Then you can divorce yourself from being the writer and approach the copy as a reader. In case you've forgotten, he's the fellow you're working for.

The Proof of the Pudding

You can't improve your writing much simply by reading a book. You have to put the ideas into practice. The key to improving one's writing is to learn to take a look at something you've written, spot where and how it could be done better, then do it. Excellent writers aren't just writers; they're writers and rewriters. Eventually a skilled writer gets so he or she can do a pretty good job on the first try. Almost always, though, he'll do a better job if you let him give it one more try.

We've discussed what I think are the most important suggestions for improving one's writing. In the rest of this book I'm going to show you how to use them. I'm going to take various pieces of writing, try to tell you what I think is wrong with them, and show you how they can be improved.

I don't claim to be right in all these cases, but, based on my experience, it's what I think should be done to improve the copy. See what you think.

Example No. 1

When Kevin Ross graduated from the eighth grade last May, his classmates selected him to deliver the commencement address to some 200 students, parents, and supporters of Chicago's Westside Preparatory School. In his address, Kevin spoke of the need to light the candle of excellence inside each individual and he told of Michelangelo holding a piece of marble and knowing that inside the stone was an angel yearning to be free.

What makes this unusual is that Kevin is 24 years old, attended college for four years, and a year ago wasn't even sure who Michelangelo was.

There are too many ideas for comfort in that first sentence. I would eliminate some and break up the following sentences with a few periods.

When Kevin Ross graduated from the eighth grade at Chicago's Westside Prep, his classmates selected him to deliver the commencement address. In his address, Kevin spoke of the need to light the candle of excellence inside each individual. He told of Michelangelo holding a piece of marble and knowing that inside the stone was an angel yearning to be free.

What makes this unusual is that Kevin was 24 years old and had already attended college for four years. A year ago he wasn't even sure who Michelangelo was.

Example No. 2

From a magazine about the economics of free enterprise. See if you can read it.

Myth shrouds the concept of industrial and professional self-regulation like a thick coastal fog, obscuring fundamental truth and casting light and shadows of chimera and deception. Analysis should disperse the fog and dispel the myth, revealing to the world the true nature of the apparition and its inherent tendencies.

Regulation necessarily implies the application of coercive force to voluntary human behavior. It consists of normative restraints upon otherwise free conduct. It matters not that the policing function derives from some or all members of an association or related group of similar businesses: the end result must be constriction of otherwise unimpeded acts—compulsion.

Attachment of the appellation "self" to the concept of regulation does little other than to disguise the concept and delude the unwary. True self-restraint presupposes internal strictures upon uninhibited courses of action, bars which stem from personal, ethical, or moral values inherent or learned. Self-regulation in the business or professional context attains quite a different picture: in place of individual assessment and determination of value rises the specter of compulsive control by the group, often engrafted into inviolate legislative principles carrying sanctions for non-compliance. Normally, a dissenter possesses no choice as to membership in the group, other than a desire to create, produce, and trade a given good, service, or idea. Once one decides to engage in a profession or an industry, he finds himself subject, as part and parcel of his activity, to the oft-Draconian codification of taboos which attend that choice. Thus, while an actor may obtain an initial choice as to market entry, self-regulation serves to circumscribe his range of choices flowing from that basic decision.

To the extent that self-regulation imposes only voluntary compliance without jural penalties, a believer in individual liberty or the doctrine of voluntarism ought take no umbrage. It is consonant with fundamental freedom to apply non-coercive peer pressure and moral suasion to inculcate right values and persuade proper conduct by one's compatriots. It is quite another thing—a malevolent matter indeed—to band together to invoke the legal processes in order to fit one's fellows unto Procrustes' bed even in the good names of morals, honor, and justice! Further analysis in this essay challenges the propriety of industrial/professional self-regulation of the coercive sort.

We're afraid the author here is too concerned with the "literary" quality of his efforts, too little aware of the problems he is creating for the reader. It's impossible to simplify material like this merely by changing a few words and eliminating others. To some extent you have to think more simply, then write more simply. See if this revision isn't a little easier to follow:

Myth and make-believe shroud the concept of industrial and professional self-regulation like a fog. They obscure the truth, and deceive the casual observer. Let's see if logical analysis can disperse this fog and reveal the true nature of most self-regulatory efforts.

Regulation implies the application of force to human behavior. It sets up standards to govern otherwise free conduct. It doesn't matter who polices these standards—either some or all of a related group—the result is compulsion.

The concept of "self"-regulation is deceptive. It does not necessarily spring, as one might assume, from the personal values of each individual or company. Self-regulation in a business or profession often represents compulsive control by a group. The rules are formulated into laws with punishments for noncompliance. Normally, a dissenter has no choice as to whether he wants to be a member of the group. He is considered to be one by nature of his business or profession.

To the extent that self-regulation imposes only voluntary compliance, a dissenter cannot complain. People have a right to use peer pressure and moral persuasion to encourage what they believe to be proper conduct. They do not, however, have the right to band together and invoke legal processes in order to force their fellow businessmen or professionals to follow their particular rules. The rest of this essay will challenge the propriety of this sort of self-regulation.

Example No. 3

From a movie review:

> *"Rumble Fish", a teenage gang film with aspirations to create its own mythology, set in what may be Tulsa, Okla., is Francis Coppola's second attempt within the year to make a mountain of a movie out of a molehill of a young-adult novel by S. E. Hinton.*

This is a typical, overstuffed newspaper lead, trying to crowd every possible fact into the first sentence. And what is a movie with aspirations to create its own mythology? Just in case it might have some meaning unknown to us, we've left it in the rewrite:

> *"Rumble Fish", a teenage gang film, is Francis Coppola's second attempt within the year to make a mountain of a movie out of a molehill of a novel by S. E. Hinton. Set in what may be Tulsa, Okla., it's a young-adult movie with aspirations to create its own mythology.*

Example No. 4

This isn't so bad:

> *On the shoulders of the executives charged with leading*

the regional companies will rest much of the responsibility not just for maintaining telephone service in America at a time when the system that made that service possible is being fragmented, but for maintaining it at the levels of excellence and reliability that have become AT&T's trademark.

But isn't this better?

Executives of the leading regional companies are responsible for maintaining telephone service in America at a time when the system which made that service possible is being fragmented. They must also maintain the excellence and reliability of service that have become AT&T's trademark.

Periods are beautiful!

Example No. 5

I am giving you the comment first in this instance because I don't want you to become too discouraged trying to read the example. It's a paragraph I found in an educational yearbook. I can't edit it because I don't understand it. If you ever find yourself writing like this, grab a passing cloud and get back to earth.

It is important to note that social purposes in the stabilization category and the modification category are similar in that, in both cases, the object of the school system's concern are current users of those desirable or undesirable behavior forms which are of interest to the system. Likewise, social purposes in the reproduction category and the replacement category are similar in that, in both cases, the object of the school system's concern are prospective users of

*desirable or undesirable behavior forms. Generally speak-
ing, when school systems try to stabilize or modify social
conditions, they are trying to influence the behavior of adults
in the community and when they seek to reproduce or
replace social conditions, they are concerned with the
behavior of youngsters.*

We see no reason why the subjects above—whatever they
are—should not be treated in a manner anyone can
understand.

Example No. 6

From a current article:

> *As a consumer, every man votes in a dollar democracy,
> casting his hard-earned money ballots for the goods,
> services, and ideas he deems most efficacious and necessary
> to satisfy his wants. In the grand name of consumer
> protection, a few individuals owning subjective views of
> what is right and good for all, and currying the political
> power to effect such goals, thwart the true desire of mankind
> in society. Simply put, the panjandrumatic champion
> decides what is best for his neighbors and exchanges his
> determination for the free choice of those less politically
> fortunate.*

Less pomp and more periods make it clearer. Please note
that we eliminate the panjandrumatic champion, who
creates more confusion here than he adds meaning.

> *As a consumer, every man votes with his dollars, spending
> them for whatever goods, services, and ideas he prefers.
> Unfortunately, there are some individuals who think they*

know what is right and best for everyone. In the guise of
consumer protection, they curry power to force these goals
on the rest of us. These pretentious characters decide what is
best for their neighbors, and eliminate free choice for anyone
who is less powerful politically, than they.

Example No. 7

From a State Department release:

President Reagan, pursuant to his authority under Section
506(a) of the Foreign Assistance Act of 1961, as amended, has
determined that:

- *An unforeseen emergency exists which requires*
  immediate military assistance to Chad;

- *The aforementioned emergency requirement cannot be*
  met under the authority of the Arms Export Control Act
  or any other law except Section 506(a) of the act.

Therefore, he has authorized . . . etc.

The expression "the aforementioned emergency requirement" is pompous legalese, totally unnecessary. The idea
to which it refers is actually in the same sentence. Much
more readable and just as precise would be: "This requirement cannot be met . . . etc."

Example No. 8

Some improvements in writing require more than
simpler words and shorter sentences. They involve
changes in concept, a different approach, or simpler, more
effective ways of getting at the same ideas.

For instance, take a look at the following excerpt from an

article by an outstanding lawyer. Considering the fact that the writer is dealing with legal problems, it's an amazingly readable presentation:

> The 1973 War Powers Resolution was passed over a presidential veto at the height of the Vietnam and Watergate controversies. By requiring congressional authorization for involvement or imminent involvement of U.S. armed forces in hostilities abroad lasting more than 60 days, whether or not such involvement constituted a "war," its congressional proponents sought to ensure "no more Vietnams" and to restore to Congress the war powers they believed had been usurped by an "imperial presidency."

> No American president, however, has accepted the restrictive vision of presidential authority contained in this resolution. Constitutional history and scholarship before the Vietnam experience support a broader presidential role. The recent differences between Congress and the president over the application of this resolution to the deployment of the American troops in Lebanon present the most important occasion to date for assessment of this resolution.

> The proper role for Congress and the president in the conduct of foreign policy has been debated throughout our history. A decade of experience under the War Powers Resolution and the benefit of a calmer atmosphere suggest that this post-Vietnam resolution may have tilted the scales too much toward Congress in this struggle.

> **Strong Support**

> It is clear in hindsight that the Vietnam War did not arise because of lack of congressional authorization. Until the 1968 Tet Offensive, U.S. involvement had strong bipartisan support on the Hill.

Anyone who doubts the early congressional support and authorization for the war, which simply mirrored the Gallup Poll, should examine the detailed memorandum on the subject prepared for the American Bar Association and inserted in the Congressional Record by Sen. Javits in 1966. Paradoxically, this congressional authorization for the war would have also met the provisions of the War Powers Resolution said to be passed to prevent such involvements in the future.

The War Powers Resolution is of doubtful constitutionality. This is hardly surprising since it was not the product of an accommodation of executive and congressional views, but rather adopted the congressional view of the appropriate balance over the constitutional objections of the incumbent president and the reservations of every subsequent president.

The 1983 Chadha decision holds the legislative veto to be an unconstitutional infringement of separation of powers. At a minimum this invalidates the legislative veto in Section 5(c) of the War Powers Resolution. More importantly, the thrust of Chadha raises serious questions as to the termination provision, central to the resolution, that would require termination of involvement in hostilities or even imminent involvement in hostilities after 60 days unless authorized by Congress. If it is unconstitutional for Congress to seek to act by simple majority vote of both houses, does this not raise, at least, serious questions about a procedure that purports to terminate the commitment of forces abroad by congressional silence?

In addition, the premises of the resolution, as spelled out in Section 2 seeking to define the constitutional war powers of the president, almost certainly err in favor of congressional authority. For example, most experts would agree that the president has independent constitutional authority to use the armed forces to protect American lives abroad, such as in an attack on an American embassy, yet such authority seems not to be included within Section 2.

Many would also urge presidential authority that extended to lesser commitments, such as peacekeeping forces, yet this and other such uses of force short of war are also excluded.

More importantly, although scholars debate the precise constitutional line, it remains a puzzle how Congress can by resolution alter the Constitution. It is elementary constitutional law, as the Supreme Court enumerated in Myers vs. United States, that the constitutional scheme of separation of powers cannot be altered by one branch or indeed by anything short of constitutional amendment. It strains credulity to believe that Congress in codifying its own version of separation of powers has struck the precise balance intended by the framers.

But how might the same facts be handled by a professional writer? Let's examine the following attempt and see.

In 1973, at the height of the Vietnam and Watergate controversies, Congress passed the War Powers Resolution. It required congressional authorization for the involvement (or imminent involvement) of U.S. armed forces in hostilities abroad lasting more than 60 days.

In effect, it told the President: "Don't start anything abroad that might last more than 60 days without Congressional approval." How the President was supposed to measure in advance the time required by each involvement, Congress failed to state.

The War Powers Resolution was passed in spite of a presidential veto, and no President since has acknowledged the restrictions on presidential authority contained in that resolution. The purpose of the resolution was, supposedly, to prevent American presidents from getting us involved in any more Vietnams. Its sponsors completely ignored the fact that Congress had been as much involved in the Vietnamese war as the President. Until the Tet Offensive in 1968, U.S. involvement had strong bipartisan support on Capitol Hill.

The proper role for Congress and for the President in the conduct of foreign policy has been debated throughout our history. But we had better settle the question sooner rather than later. Can you imagine a court fight over constitutionality of the War Powers Resolution in the midst of a foreign crisis? Our possible enemies should know, very clearly and definitely, who in America has the power to do what.

The constitutionality of the War Powers Resolution is extremely doubtful. It is not a compromise of executive and congressional viewpoints. It represents the viewpoint of Congress alone as to the proper balance of power between itself and the President.

The Supreme Court's Chadha decision in 1983 said a legislative veto is an unconstitutional infringement of the doctrine of separation of powers. At the very least, this invalidates the legislative veto proposed in Section 5(c) of the War Powers Resolution. It also raises serious questions about the provisions that would require termination of involvement in hostilities. If Congress wants to legislate something, it must have a majority vote of two houses and the approval of the President. How can it be allowed to terminate hostilities simply by remaining silent?

Most experts agree that, despite the War Powers Resolution, the President has constitutional authority to use the armed forces to protect American lives abroad. Many also urge that the presidential authority should be extended to lesser commitments, such as peacekeeping forces. Yet these and other such uses are made questionable and tentative by the War Powers Resolution.

It is a puzzle to many experts how Congress can expect to change the Constitution by a simple resolution. It is elementary constitutional law that the separation of powers cannot be altered by any one branch of government or by anything short of a constitutional amendment.

There—doesn't that sound a little more readable? Perhaps in the next generation we should cross lawyers with writers.

Example No. 9

Here's a message for supervisors, very simple and straightforward:

When you have an idea that's perfectly clear to you, it ought to be easy to make it perfectly clear to someone else. Right? Wrong. One of the most costly, needless mistakes a supervisor can make is to assume people understand when they don't. Yet it happens time and again.

Why does an idea that's crystal clear in your mind get mixed up by the person you tell it to? One reason is that the words you use mean one thing to you and something else to the person you are talking to. Even when you talk in terms your listeners understand, you may still have trouble getting your message across. If they have strong opinions or preconceived notions about what you are saying, your idea could easily be distorted.

Another thing to watch for: are they really listening? If they have something else on their minds, they may listen to what you say without really hearing it. Make certain your message isn't going in one ear and out the other. Unfortunately, you can't really tell if your message gets through just by asking your listener: "Do you understand?" The person who heard your message certainly understood something. But how do you know if it was the idea you wanted to communicate?

Lots of employees simply won't admit it when they don't get your message. They think you'll get mad if they ask you to explain again. So they take a chance that they got your idea. And often end up by doing just what you didn't want done.

The one sure way of finding out if your listeners are tuned in to your message is to ask them to play it back to you—in their own words. You'll know right away if you got through. And you could prevent a mistake before it happens.

Don't take chances. Make sure all your messages get through straight. Follow up and ask people to play them back. Make them prove they understand exactly what you mean. If you leave any chance for error, some day there'll be one. You can count on it!

Perfectly clear! No gobbledygook there. Just for the fun of it, though, take a look at the identical message illustrated with a few cartoons to help drive home each point. This is how it appeared in an issue of Better Supervision.

"IT WAS OBVIOUS...
HOW COULD ANYONE MISUNDERSTAND?"

When you have an idea that's perfectly clear to you, it ought to be easy to make it perfectly clear to somebody else. Right?

Wrong.

One of the most costly, needless mistakes a supervisor can make is to assume people understand when they don't. Yet it happens time and again.

Why does an idea that's crystal
clear in your mind get mixed up
by the person you tell it to? One
reason is that the words you
use mean one thing to you and
something else to the person
you're talking to.

"GET ME
A SMALL BOX."

Even when you talk in terms
your listeners understand, you
may still have trouble getting
your message across. If they
have strong opinions or
preconceived notions about what
you are saying, your idea could
easily be distorted.

"HE SAYS
IT'S A RUSH JOB!"

"EVERYTHING'S
A RUSH JOB!"

"THIS ISN'T WHAT I WANTED..."

Another thing to watch for:
are they really listening? If they
have something else on their
minds, they may *listen* to what
you say without really *hearing*
it. Make certain your message
isn't going in one ear and
out the other.

"HE SAID HE UNDERSTOOD!" "BUT HE OBVIOUSLY DIDN'T."

Unfortunately, you can't really tell if your message gets through just by asking your listener: "Do you understand?" The person who heard your message certainly understood something. But how do you know if it was the idea you wanted to communicate?

Lots of employees simply won't
admit it when they don't get
your message. They think you'll
get mad if they ask you to
explain again. So they take a
chance that they got your idea.
And often end up by doing just
what you didn't want done.

"ISN'T THAT WHAT YOU WANTED?"

"NO...NOT AT ALL."

The one sure way of finding
out if your listeners are tuned
in to your message is to ask
them to play it back to you—in
their own words. You'll know
right away if you got through.
And you could prevent a mistake
before it happens.

Don't take chances. Make sure
all your messages get through
straight. Follow up and ask
people to play them back. Make
them *prove* they understand
exactly what you mean. If you
leave any chance for error,
someday there'll be one. You
can count on it!

Don't you think it's a stronger, clearer message with the drawings than without? Cartoons and drawings cost money, but they do illustrate the point you're trying to make and definitely make the reading more inviting. Don't forget, we all grew up on a diet of comic books. Most of us haven't gotten over it yet.

A number of years ago I wrote a book about handling people called *"Let's Be Human"*. To trap foremen and supervisors into reading it, the people I really wanted to reach, I put a cartoon and only one or two sentences of text on every page. Every idea was illustrated with humor. So what happened? It became a selection of the Executive Book Club! You never know, do you?

Example No. 10

A successful business executive is usually a practical person; he or she knows how to get things done. A professor is more often a theoretical person. He likes to consider things from every possible angle and often uses complex, complicated language to do it. The obvious conclusion: when a professor writes something he hopes business executives will read and act upon, he had better keep it simple. Otherwise executives will read it reluctantly, with skepticism, or perhaps not read it at all.

The other day a friend of mine, the president of a very successful small company, handed me a copy of a new book about employee incentive programs. "This doesn't interest me," he said. "It's too theoretical, too complex. Maybe you can get something out of it."

So I read it—or at least waded through part of it—just to

see what it was all about. Actually, the subject matter was something my business executive friend would have been tremendously interested in if it had been expressed in simpler, more understandable terms. Instead, the message was buried under a sea of complicated expressions like microvariables, macrovariables, rationales, overviews, philosophical and behavioral differences, diagnostic management tools, formula implementation, behavioral and organizational factors, and the area of economic flexibility and cyclical variation.

I won't attempt to tell you what these words mean (in some cases I'm not quite sure) or what words the authors should have used in place of them. What I will say is that the same ideas could have been expressed in much simpler, more interesting fashion without using any of them. And all of mankind would be better off as a result.

To give you a better idea of how hard the text was to read in some places, here are a few paragraphs:

Value-Added (Rucker) Formula

Figure 3-3 illustrates the value-added, or Rucker, formula as it interacts with the behavioral and organizational factors. The relative strength of its reinforcement value is equal to the single and split ratio formulas. The base of cooperation is equal to scanlon-type formulas if involvement systems accompany this formula.

In fact, most of the behavioral and organizational factors have similar profiles to those in the single and split ratio formulas. The key differences are in the area of economic flexibility and cyclical variation. Most scanlon formulas do not deal well with the inflationary effects on the sales value of production. Double-digit inflation can undermine the appropriateness of base ratio of most scanlon calculations.

Value-added formulas subtract outside purchases (material and supplies, energy, etc.) from the sales value of production to determine the value added by the production process. Based on historical data, allowed labor costs are computed as a percentage of the value added. This ratio is then multiplied by the value added in a particular period and compared to actual labor costs.

Had enough? Instead of rewriting anything they said, let's simply look at how another author writes about the same subject. He is Frederick G. Lesieur, an authority on the Scanlon Plan for increasing productivity.

One of the greatest advantages of this kind of collective bargaining from the worker's point of view, is the knowledge that it gives him of the business. When a slump is coming, he knows it. He is even given a chance to combat it, in the sense that if he can devise a cheaper way of turning out his product, perhaps the company will be able to take away business from somebody else.

In a number of instances the Lapointe workers have actually done this, the most spectacular example being that of an order from a big automotive concern. The workers had been pressing management to accept orders even at the break-even point so as to tide over a bad period. Mr. Prindiville, who sometimes sits in on the screening-committee meetings, had given in to the pressure some months previously to the extent of taking an order from this firm for 100 broaches at $83 per broach. But Lapointe had lost 10 percent on the deal, and Mr. Prindiville now put his foot down. If this business was to be taken again the price *would have to be raised. In view of new competition, it meant that Lapointe almost certainly would not get the business—at a time when work was scarce.*

The gloomy gathering that listened to Mr. Prindiville's pronouncement was then electrified by a question from Jimmie McQuade, skilled grinder and one of the most outspoken members of the screening committee. Who says we can't make those broaches at that price for a profit? Mr. McQuade wanted to know. If you'd give the men in the shop a chance to go over the blueprints before production starts and to help plan the job, there are lots of ways of cutting costs without cutting quality. The idea grew, and the next day the suggestion ran around the shop like wildfire. The order was taken at the old price, this time with a profit of 10 percent—a total gain in efficiency of 20 percent.

The truth is that the Scanlon Plan has generated a competitive spirit throughout the factory: one hears as much about competition from the workers as from management itself. If there is a question of struggling for existence the whole company struggles collectively, and all the brains available are focused on the fight. The worker is no longer a pawn in a game he does not understand. He is a player. He enjoys it. And his contribution is worth money to all concerned.

Widespread interest in the Scanlon Plan is a result not merely of the merits of the plan itself. It also owes a great deal to Mr. Lesieur's ability to present the plan in a manner anyone can easily read and understand.

Example No. 11

Have you ever noticed that when a piece of writing is

unusually clear—a cinch to read and understand—the writer has usually expressed his ideas in more than one way? He keeps adding explanatory remarks, saying the same thing in different words, to give the reader a better chance to grasp his meaning. That's what people do when they're talking together. Why not do it the same way when you're writing something?

In case you didn't notice, this is exactly what I've done twice in the preceding paragraph. The expression "a cinch to read and understand" amplifies and reexpresses the idea of "unusually clear". "Saying the same thing in different words" is another way of saying "explanatory remarks".

Never hesitate to say the same thing twice, especially if you can do it quickly and briefly. Very few of us have lightning-speed brains. Most people appreciate a second chance to grab and digest the meaning.

Take a look, for example, at the following excerpt from a booklet called "THINK!". Compared with some of the samples we've dissected here, you'll find it very easy reading. Like rolling off a log.

There is no monopoly on the ability to think. Thinkers may occur at any level of business . . . from errand boy to president. They are the kind of people who can't help wondering about what they are doing . . . whether it's really necessary . . . and whether there isn't a better way to do it. Thinkers are the yeast that makes a business grow . . . the prod in the backside that keeps an organization awake and moving.

Why the difference between thinkers and nonthinkers? What makes them that way? Lord only knows! But one thing is obvious: the difference is not as much a problem of brain structure as it is a fundamental difference in habit, attitude, and training.

Most people, simply by applying a few sound principles—by using the right methods—could think more effectively than they do. They could make better, wiser decisions at home and at work. They could earn more money and spend it more wisely. They could find more right answers to their personal problems, fewer wrong ones.

Why is the foregoing article so easy to read and understand? Because the writer keeps repeating ideas in other words and giving examples of those ideas. Take another look at the article that we've reproduced again below. The repetition and examples of ideas previously expressed are underlined. As soon as the writer says anything, he starts clarifying and illustrating it.

There is no monopoly on the ability to think. Thinkers may occur at any level of business . . . from errand boy to president. They are the kind of people who can't help wondering about what they are doing . . . whether it's really necessary . . . and whether there isn't a better way to do it. Thinkers are the yeast that makes a business grow . . . the prod in the backside that keeps an organization awake and moving.

Why the difference between thinkers and nonthinkers? What makes them that way? Lord only knows! But one thing is obvious: the difference is not as much a problem of brain structure as it is a fundamental difference in habit, attitude, and training.

Most people, simply by applying a few sound principles—by using the right methods—could think more effectively than they do. *They could make better, wiser decisions at home and at work. They could earn more money and spend it more wisely. They could find more right answers to their personal problems, fewer wrong ones.*

Example No. 12

The following three paragraphs were submitted to a group of executives serving as an advisory council to a university business school. This statement, labeled "Program Philosophy", is probably of average complexity for such documents. It's only three paragraphs long, so don't get too discouraged. When you've finished, we'll take a look, sentence by sentence, to see if there's anything we can do to make it easier to read and to understand.

I. PROGRAM PHILOSOPHY

The fundamental premise upon which both the undergraduate and MBA programs are based is that the successful practice of the art of management requires the ability to recognize and adapt to an environment which is constantly changing in ways which are difficult if not impossible to correctly anticipate. The nature of the optimal solution to any particular problem facing management is constantly being altered as the environment in which the organization operates evolves. Approaches which are optimal today will be suboptimal next year. Indeed, the problems themselves are different from one period to the next. The development of managerial techniques and the success of any individual manager is a process of natural selection: the survival of a manager is a function of the ability to recognize change and adapt techniques as quickly and as appropriately as possible. Those who anticipate best and adapt fastest will dominate.

Programs that concentrate on the procedural as opposed to the conceptual aspects of managerial decision-making cannot possibly prepare an individual for a world such as this. If successful adaptation to change is to be due to anything other than pure chance, the manager must be firmly grounded in the science upon which the art of management is based.

The School has responded by offering professional course work which is built upon the mathematical, natural, and social sciences. At the undergraduate level, the School of Business Administration requires a strong general education core in the freshman and sophomore years which encourages the students to broaden their horizons and develop their powers of logical reasoning and imaginative thought as fully as possible. The professional course work offered in the junior and senior years builds upon this base in all functional areas of management, developing normative principles for the decision-making process.

Okay, let's start with the first sentence.

The fundamental premise upon which both the under-graduate and MBA programs are based is that the successful practice of the art of management requires the ability to recognize and adapt to an environment which is constantly changing in ways which are difficult if not impossible to correctly anticipate.

How would it sound if we knocked out a few nonessential words and broke it into two sentences? For example:

The premise upon which both the undergraduate and MBA programs are based is that successful management requires the ability to recognize and adapt to a constantly

*changing environment. These changes are difficult, some-
times impossible, to anticipate.*

Then sentences no. 2, 3, and 4:

*The nature of the optimal solution to any particular
problem facing management is constantly being altered as
the environment in which the organization operates evolves.
Approaches which are optimal today will be suboptimal next
year. Indeed the problems themselves are different from one
period to the next.*

Instead of improving these sentences, why don't we try a
simpler approach to the same ideas:

*The best answer to a management problem this year may
not be the best answer next year. Problems and answers
change constantly, along with the changing environment in
which an organization operates.*

As for the last two sentences of paragraph 1, we'd say it
this way:

*The development of managerial techniques and the
progress of individual managers is a matter of natural
selection. The manager who adopts the most successful
techniques the soonest moves ahead the fastest.*

Now for paragraph no. 2. The difficulty here is that I'm
not sure exactly what the writer was driving at. I hope you
will agree that this is not entirely my fault. I would reword
it as follows:

*Programs which concentrate solely on the procedures for
making management decisions cannot prepare an individual
for the modern business world. Managers must also be*

grounded in the general and scientific knowledge necessary to be sure such decisions are correct.

Now for the last paragraph. We don't have many changes and they are not too vital, so we'll just reproduce the paragraph as edited below:

The School has faced this problem by offering professional course work which builds on the student's previous exposure to mathematical, natural, and social sciences. At the undergraduate level, the School of Business Administration requires a strong general education core in freshman and sophomore years which encourages students to broaden their horizons. During these two years we try to develop their powers of logical reasoning and imaginative thought. The professional course work offered in the junior and senior years builds upon this base and develops guiding principles for making business decisions.

I'm sure this editing process has been a bit confusing. Now, however, let's put the pieces together and see how the result would read. Here is our rewritten version of the complete message.

I. PROGRAM PHILOSOPHY

The premise upon which both the undergraduate and MBA programs are based is that successful management requires the ability to recognize and adapt to a constantly changing environment. These changes are difficult, sometimes impossible, to anticipate. The best answer to a management problem this year may not be the best answer next year. Problems and answers change constantly, along with the changing environment in which an organization operates.

The development of managerial techniques and the progress of individual managers is a matter of natural selection. The manager who adopts the most successful techniques the soonest moves ahead the fastest.

Programs which concentrate solely on the procedures for making management decisions cannot prepare an individual for the modern business world. Managers must also be grounded in the general and scientific knowledge necessary to be sure such decisions are correct.

The School has faced this problem by offering professional course work which builds on the student's previous exposure to mathematical, natural, and social sciences. At the undergraduate level, the School of Business Administration requires a strong general education core in freshman and sophomore years which encourages students to broaden their horizons. During these two years we try to develop their powers of logical reasoning and imaginative thought. The professional course work offered in the junior and senior years builds upon this base and develops guiding principles for making business decisions.

Now, in case you've forgotten what it sounded like, turn back a few pages and read the original version again. Which do you like better? Whichever it is, good luck to you. Go thou and do likewise!

Example No. 13

People being people, one might expect a statement of policy for a school of business to sound a bit ethereal and statesmanlike. The writer couldn't resist the temptation to do a little high-level sounding off regardless of whether anyone understood it or not. Unfortunately, some people let the same tone creep into ordinary business correspondence. Can you imagine a letter like the following? It was written by a salesman looking for some printing business and addressed to the executive vice president of a company he had never contacted before.

Dear Mr. Jones:

Would that my initial contact with you and your organization could be promoted through mutual acquaintance, business or professional: the confidence factor would have to be enhanced, in addition to my certainty of addressing the correct individual(s) with our services. However, given exceptional competitive leverage of a "city" typesetting/printing supplier without city overhead encourages me to present Segar & Wiate. Logistics defer my personally contacting and visiting you for a week or two; in the interim, I invite immediate response via samples and specifications. I will be following up as quickly as possible in any eventuality.

We are a totally self-contained full service printer. We work around the clock to respond to critical, demanding typesetting and printing schedules. Turnaround is same day or overnight as required and we are staffed and equipped for telecommunications, facsimile transmissions, and immediate pick-up and delivery. This, of course, qualifies us to handle regulatory printing. A variety of descriptive brochures further specifies our capabilities.

We have established an enviable record of service to our customers while maintaining very competitive prices. I look forward to hearing from you or as indicated, I will be in touch with you.

> *Very truly yours,*
>
> *Segar and Wiate, Printers*

The ridiculous part of this letter is the first paragraph. The rest of it isn't so bad. It does, however, express far too many ideas in terms of "we" instead of talking in terms of "you".

We can't help but feel that a simple, straightforward, unpretentious note would have made a far better impression. Something like the following:

I wish, Mr. Jones,

that we had a close mutual friend. Then he could tell you— and you could believe—what an excellent printing organization we operate. He could also tell me whom in your organization I should call on to present our abilities to be of service.

Lacking such a friend, I'm appealing directly to you. I suspect Segar & Wiate printing services might be excellent for your needs. We are a totally self-contained, full-service printer and we work around the clock. Our services are available any time you need them. Turnaround is the same day or overnight, and we are staffed and equipped for telecommunications, facsimile transmissions, and, of course, immediate pick up and delivery.

I will be in touch with you shortly to see whom you would like me to approach to describe our services and learn of your needs in this area. I think it might be a very productive meeting for both of us.

Sincerely,

Segar and Wiate, Printers

Even in business, people are still people. They should write, talk, and act like friendly individuals, not inanimate objects.

In Conclusion

I had intended to use another example here, but in searching for an appropriate piece I became obsessed with an idea that has bugged me for years. Perhaps you've had enough examples by now. How about a few biased opinions instead?

In looking for some complicated writing to simplify, I asked a friend who has a good library and likes to read what he would recommend. "I have just the thing for you," he said. "It's a book that was on the recommended reading list in my sociology course in college. I tried, but I couldn't make myself read it. You practically had to decipher it sentence by sentence. It wasn't worth the effort so I never finished it."

He gave me the book and I spent several hours with it, reading sections here and there. It was a saddening experience. The man was brilliant. The ideas that poked through his complicated language were interesting—what I could decipher of them. But who wants to decipher? Complex words and ideas were jammed in with other difficult concepts—without adequate repetition, explanation or soaking time. It was hard to get and keep the train of thought.

If the professor had written his book in simple English, I'd have been fascinated by it. Instead, he wrote it in sociological gobbledygook. It was intended, I'm afraid, not to interest and educate ordinary people like my friend and me, but to impress other professionals in the field. What a waste!

I read another tedious book a year or so ago because it contained some information I sorely needed. The language was painfully erudite and I had to push myself to continue. Suddenly I came across an expression I wasn't familiar with, "in the praxis". Picking up a dictionary I found it meant the same thing as "in practice". But who in the world would bother to use the expression? Except, perhaps, to impress others with his intellectual qualifications. Certainly not to communicate better.

Over the years each of us develops certain beliefs and prejudices. For example, if a person cannot explain his viewpoint well enough for me to understand it, I begin to suspect he doesn't know what he is talking about. A very egotistical view, but I've found it's true more often than untrue. I tend to have little faith in people who can't use simple English to say what they mean.

Everyone—professors, scientists, doctors, sociologists—should learn how to write and speak ordinary, everyday language. They should learn how to communicate with ordinary people. Then the common people might not be so common. They would have a chance to understand more of the wonders of this world instead of being kept in the outer darkness. Professional language may be all right when you're talking to another professional, but it's also possible to find a way to say the same thing in ordinary language. A lot of us would deeply appreciate it if you did.